TOFU
Quick & Easy

by Louise Hagler

The Book Publishing Company • Summertown, Tennessee 38483

Production Editor:
Louise Hagler

Food Stylist:
Louise Hagler

Photography:
Michael Bonnickson

Acknowledgements:

Special thanks to Dorothy Bates for her support and many recipe contributions, to Marjorie Curry for her support and many dishes for our pictures, to Bob and Cynthia Holzapfel and Richard Martin for their help in production, to the Cook's Nook in Nashville for dishes and picture props, and to my family, without whose help this book would still not be finished.

This book is dedicated to my mother who taught me
to not be afraid to try new and different food.

On the cover: Spinach Pine-Nut Salad, page 30, Stuffed Jumbo Shells, page 62, Cheesecake, page 84

Hagler, Louise
  Tofu quick & easy

  Includes index.
  1. Cookery (Tofu)   I. Title.   II. Title: Tofu quick and easy.
  III. Title: Tofu.
TX814.5.T63H34   1988   641.6'5655   87-34123

ISBN 0-913990-50-7 (pbk.)

  3 4 5 6 7 8 9 0

Copyright © 1986 The Book Publishing Company, Summertown, Tennessee 38483

TABLE OF CONTENTS

Breakfast or Brunch ♦ 9

Dips and Spreads ♦ 19

Salads and Salad Dressings ♦ 27

Soups ♦ 45

Main Dishes ♦ 55

Desserts ♦ 83

Introduction

Tofu has recently found its way into our western supermarkets after having been an Asian protein staple for 2,000 years. The question many people ask now is "What do I do with it?". The answer is here in the "quick and easy" form for today's cook, who wants to prepare a delicious meal without spending hours in the kitchen.

Tofu is one of the most versatile and economical protein foods there is. It is high in protein and low in calories, fats and carbohydrates. This white, bland-tasting soft block of quality vegetable protein has the potential of being turned into anything from tasty main dishes and side dishes, salads and salad dressings, dips, spreads, sauces and soups to delectable desserts. Tofu assumes whatever flavor is added to it. Whip up Pesto Dip (page 25) for your next party appetizer, or Garlic Lo-Cal Dressing (page 43) for a salad. Delight in an Ensalada de Aguacate (page 29). Sink your teeth into Barbecue Tofu (page 57). Savor Corn Chowder (page 47) or choose from several different and luscious cheesecakes (pages 84-85).

Nutritive Values

Tofu is a wholesome, complete vegetable protein that is very easy to digest. This makes it a good food for babies, children and the elderly. It is an excellent food for sensitive stomachs and a perfect protein food for those with heart disease because it has no cholesterol. Those who are allergic to milk or eggs, or those who follow strict dietary laws prohibiting dairy products find that tofu adds great variety to their menus.

Tofu is as growth-promoting as meat or dairy products. In 120 grams of tofu (this is a little over ¼ lb.) there are: 9.4 grams of protein, 5 grams fat, 2.9 grams carbohydrates, 154 mg. potassium, and small amounts of niacin, riboflavin and thiamine. In this same 120 grams of tofu there are only 86 calories.* Tofu contains all essential amino acids for the body's energy and protein needs.

Cooking Time

The recipes in this book all take less than 30 minutes to prepare. In some cases the cooking time will take longer, but in many cases the whole recipe can be ready to eat in 15 minutes or less. Everyone works at a different pace. A beginning cook might take a little longer than an experienced one, and some people like to work at a more leisurely pace than others. Before you start, be sure to read through a recipe to have a clear idea of what the procedure is. A microwave oven can be used to speed up cooking for casseroles that only need to be heated. I have only given conventional oven cooking times because each brand of microwave has a little different power and settings. As you are familiar with your own type of microwave oven, you will be able to convert the times and settings.

I hope that this book will introduce you to cooking with tofu in a way that makes you feel like it is your old familiar food friend and that tofu will become a regular part of your menus.

*From USDA *Composition of Foods*

Care & Handling

Tofu is available in several different forms, ranging from a very soft silken tofu to a very firm, hard-pressed and sliceable cheese. The protein content of tofu varies depending on how dense it is and the amount of water it contains — the firmer the tofu, the higher the protein content. Also, the firmer the tofu, the better it is for slicing or cubing. The softer tofu lends itself more to mashing or blending.

Purchasing Tofu

Really fresh tofu has barely any scent at all. It has a slightly sweet, mild vegetable smell. When buying tofu, look for the freshest possible, checking the expiration date on the package. If the tofu is not vacuum packed, gently rinse it under cold water when you bring it home, then store it covered with cold water in the refrigerator. If you rinse it and change the water every day, it can keep up to two weeks. If mold becomes visible, or it turns a pinkish color, or becomes slimy, throw it out. Tofu can still be used if it has a slightly sour smell, but it must be cooked for at least 20 minutes. This can be done by boiling it in water, which changes it to a harder and chewier texture, or by using it in a recipe that calls for at least 20 minutes baking time. Slightly sour tofu makes a fine baked cheesecake. Give your tofu the sniff test daily when you change the water. If I can't use my tofu right away when it starts to smell a little sour, I put it in the freezer to use later. Use only the freshest tofu for recipes that call for no cooking. If the tofu you buy smells sour when you open it, or looks pink or bubbly, take it back to your grocer for a replacement and recommend that he keep it at a cooler temperature.

Measuring Tofu

Tofu generally comes in one pound packages. A pound of tofu is equal to two cups. If you need to measure, the water displacement method works well. To measure ½ lb. tofu, fill a 4 cup measuring cup to the 3 cup level, then add a piece of tofu or enough slices or cubes to bring the water level up to the 4 cup mark. You will get to where you can estimate pretty easily.

Marinating Tofu

Marinades and tofu work together very well. With meats, marinating is usually done to tenderize as well as add flavor.

Since tofu is already tender, a long marinating time is not necessary. Sometimes a little time is needed for the flavors to soak in and blend. If the tofu is to be cooked, the cooking will bring out the flavors of the marinade. Marinating should always be done in glass, stainless steel or enamel. A flat pan works best for marinating slices or cubes. Turn the pieces several times or use a turkey baster to suck up and squirt the marinade over the pieces. To avoid the risk of bacterial growth, marinating should be done in the refrigerator.

Useful Kitchen Tools

There are several kitchen tools that are helpful in cooking with tofu. A food processor or blender are essential. Either one will work well in these recipes, although some food processors will not make as creamy a product as a blender. A food processor is more efficient because it will generally blend all ingredients at once, whereas a blender may require several batches. To save wear and tear on your blender motor, a good rule to follow is to only blend ½ lb. of tofu at a time. You can mix all the ingredients for a recipe together in a bowl, then blend one cup at a time in the blender. Stir all your blender batches together at the end. Also, with a blender, you may have to add a little more liquid than the recipe calls for and you may have to coax the blending along, oh so carefully, with a rubber spatula. An electric mixer can be used to blend the softer tofu for dips, dressings and spreads.

If you lack these kitchen power tools, the softest of tofu can be blended with a wire whip.

Freezing Tofu

Freezing your tofu changes it to a more chewy, meaty consistency. It can be frozen right in the package or each block wrapped in plastic or foil. Before using it, it must be thawed and squeezed out. It will resemble a spongy latticework, which soaks up marinade and sauces more readily than the fresh form. When it is frozen, tofu changes color from white to light tan. To thaw frozen tofu, remember to take it out of the freezer ahead of time. It takes 6 to 8 hours to defrost at room temperature, or overnight in the refrigerator. For fast defrosting, pour boiling water over it as needed, or use the microwave oven.

Breakfast or Brunch

Apple Kuchen ◆ 12
Apple Pancakes ◆ 12
Blueberry Pancakes ◆ 12
Boofers ◆ 16
Broccoli Quiche ◆ 10
Fried Rice with Tofu ◆ 13
Hash Browns ◆ 16
Mexicali Rice Bake ◆ 15
Mushroom Quiche ◆ 10
Mushroom Scrambled Tofu ◆ 14
Pancakes ◆ 12
Scrambled Tofu ◆ 14
Scrambled Tofu Rancheros ◆ 15
Spanish Rice ◆ 11

Broccoli Quiche

Yield: 6 servings

See photo on back cover.

Preheat oven to 350° F.

Boil in 1 inch of water for 5 minutes:
3 cups broccoli flowerettes, drain

Saute together:
**2 Tbsp. oil
1 cup onion, chopped
3 cloves garlic, minced**

Blend together in a food processor or blender until smooth and creamy:
**½ lb. tofu
2 Tbsp. lemon juice
1 Tbsp. dry mustard
1 tsp. salt
¼ tsp. black pepper**

Fold in:
**½ lb. tofu, crumbled
the onions and garlic
the broccoli flowerettes**

Bake in an oiled 9″ pie pan for about 30 minutes and serve hot.

Per Serving: Calories: 242, Protein: 10 gm., Fat: 12 gm., Carbohydrates: 18 gm.

Mushroom Quiche

Yield: 6 servings

A moist tender quiche with subtle flavors.

Preheat oven to 375° F.

Have ready:
1 unbaked 8″ pie shell

Saute in a skillet until slightly browned:
1 Tbsp. oil or margarine
4 oz. mushrooms, sliced

Blend in a food processor until creamy:
1 lb. tofu
2 Tbsp. lemon juice
1 Tbsp. soy sauce
1 Tbsp. Dijon mustard
½ tsp. garlic powder

Line the bottom of the pie shell with the browned mushrooms.

Fold into the tofu mixture:
2 oz. Swiss cheese, grated

Pour and spread all into the pie shell and bake 50 to 55 minutes.

Per Serving: Calories: 230, Protein: 10 gm., Fat: 12 gm., Carbohydrates: 13 gm.

Spanish Rice

Yield: 6 cups

This is a traditional Spanish rice with the additional protein of tofu.

Stir over medium heat until it starts to brown:
2 Tbsp. oil
1½ cups uncooked long grain white rice

Pour in:
2 cups boiling water
1 cup picante sauce (your choice how hot)
½ lb. tofu, cut in short julienne strips or crumbled
½ tsp. salt

Cover and cook over high heat until it starts to boil, then turn down to low heat and cook covered for 15-20 minutes until rice is tender. Serve.

Per 1 Cup Serving: Calories: 224, Protein: 6 gm., Fat: 5 gm., Carbohydrates: 36 gm.

Pancakes

Yield: 10-12 3" pancakes

Mix together in a bowl:
 2 cups biscuit mix
 ½ lb. tofu, crumbled
 1½ cups milk (more for thinner pancakes)

Cook pancakes on a hot oiled griddle until browned on both sides. Serve with margarine or butter and syrup.

Per Pancake: Calories: 121, Protein: 5 gm., Fat: 1 gm., Carbohydrates: 19 gm.

Apple Pancakes: Fold in **1 cup grated apple.**
Blueberry Pancakes: Fold in **1 cup blueberries.**

Apple Kuchen

Yield: 6 servings

Preheat oven to 375° F.

Blend in a food processor or blender until smooth:
 ½ lb. tofu
 ⅓ cup sugar
 ¼ cup flour
 1 Tbsp. oil
 ½ tsp. baking powder

Stir in:
 1 cup apples, peeled and chopped
 ½ cup chopped walnuts

Spread in an oiled 9" pie pan, sprinkle with cinnamon and bake 45-50 minutes. Cut in 6 wedges. Serve hot.

Per Serving: Calories: 185, Protein: 6 gm., Fat: 8 gm., Carbohydrates: 20 gm.

Fried Rice with Tofu

Yield: 6 cups

A good way to use leftover rice.

Have ready:
> **2 cups cooked rice**
> **1 large onion, sliced**
> **1 green pepper, sliced**
> **2 ribs celery, sliced**
> **½ lb. tofu, diced**
> **2 green onions, cut in ½" pieces**

Heat in a skillet or wok:
> **2 Tbsp. oil**

Add and stir fry for 1 minute:
> **the tofu cubes**
> **1 Tbsp. soy sauce**

Remove tofu and stir fry 3-4 minutes:
> **2 Tbsp. oil**
> **the onion slices**
> **the green pepper slices**
> **the celery slices**

Crumble in:
> **the cooked rice**

Add:
> **1 Tbsp. soy sauce**
> **the cooked tofu cubes**

Stir fry until hot. Serve sprinkled with:
> **the chopped green onion**

Per 1 Cup Serving: Calories: 204 gm., Protein: 5 gm., Fat: 9 gm., Carbohydrates: 22 gm.

Scrambled Tofu

Yield: 3 cups

Heat in a skillet or wok:
> **2 Tbsp. oil**

Stir in:
> **1 small onion, chopped (½ cup)**
> **1 small green pepper, chopped (1 cup)**
> **1 lb. tofu, crumbled**
> **2 Tbsp. nutritional yeast (optional)**
> **1 tsp. salt**
> **½ tsp. poultry seasoning**
> **½ tsp. garlic powder**
> **¼ tsp. black pepper**

Stir and fry until tofu starts to brown. Serve with toast or rice.

Per 1 Cup Serving: Calories: 212, Protein: 13 gm., Fat: 9 gm., Carbohydrates: 7 gm.

Mushroom Scrambled Tofu

Yield: 3 cups

Heat in a skillet or wok:
> **2 Tbsp. oil**

Stir in:
> **1 cup mushrooms, sliced**
> **½ cup onions, chopped**
> > **or 1 Tbsp. onion powder**
> **1 lb. tofu, crumbled**
> **1 clove garlic, minced,**
> > **or ¼ tsp. garlic powder**

When tofu starts to brown stir in:
> **1 Tbsp. soy sauce**
> **1 Tbsp. fresh parsley, chopped**

Serve with rice, noodles or toast.

Per 1 Cup Serving: Calories: 215, Protein: 13 gm., Fat: 9 gm., Carbohydrates: 8 gm.

Scrambled Tofu Rancheros

3MAY92
√√√

Yield: 3½ cups

Heat in a skillet or wok:
   2 Tbsp. oil

Stir in:
   1 small onion, chopped (½ cup)
   1 lb. tofu, crumbled
   1 clove garlic, minced
      or ½ tsp. garlic powder

Cook and stir for 5 minutes then stir in:
   1 large tomato, chopped (1 ½ cup)
   2 Tbsp. fresh parsley, chopped
   1-4 oz. can green chilies, chopped, drained
   1 tsp. salt

Stir and cook until tofu starts to brown.

Serve hot with hot corn tortillas. Pass the salsa.

Per 1 Cup Filling: Calories: 186, Protein: 11 gm., Fat: 8 gm., Carbohydrates: 7 gm.

Mexicali Rice Bake

Yield: 6 cups

Mix together and put into a 1½ quart oiled baking dish:
   3½ cups cooked rice
   2 cups Mock Sour Cream Dressing, p. 42
   4 oz. Monterey Jack cheese, grated
      (reserve enough to sprinkle over the top)
   2-4 oz. cans green chiles, drained and chopped
   4-5 drops cayenne sauce (optional)

Sprinkle reserved cheese over the top and bake 15 to 20 minutes to heat through and melt the cheese on top. Baking takes longer when starting with cold rice.

Per 1 Cup Serving: Calories: 383, Protein: 10 gm., Fat: 21 gm., Carbohydrates: 31 gm.

Boofers

See photo, page 17.

Have ready:
   3 cups mashed potatoes from instant mashed, according to directions

Saute together:
   1 Tbsp. oil
   1 medium onion, chopped

Mix into the potatoes along with:
   ½ lb. tofu, crumbled
   ¼ cup parsely, minced
   ½ tsp. salt
   ¼ tsp. black pepper

Shape into 12 patties ½" thick and brown about 4 minutes each side in:
   2 Tbsp. oil

Per Patty: Calories: 83, Protein: 3 gm., Fat: 4 gm., Carbohydrates: 8 gm.

Hash Browns

Heat in a skillet:
   ¼ cup oil

Add:
   1 lb. frozen Southern Style Hash Browns

Cover and stir a few times to thaw, then add:
   ½ cup onion, chopped
   ½ lb. tofu, crumbled
   1 tsp. salt
   ¼ tsp. black pepper

Continue to cook covered until they start to brown, then turn to brown the other side. It will not hold together in one unit. Serve hot.

Per 1 Cup Serving: Calories: 250, Protein: 7 gm., Fat: 14 gm., Carbohydrates: 20 gm.

Boofers (this page)

Dips and Spreads

Blue Cheese Spread ♦ 24
Cashew Spread ♦ 21
Cucumber Dill Dip ♦ 24
Curry Chutney Dip ♦ 22
Dry Onion Soup Dip ♦ 22
Dry Onion-Tomato Soup Dip ♦ 22
Dry Vegetable Soup Dip ♦ 22
Far East Dip ♦ 21
Green Dip or Spread ♦ 20
Green Goddess Dip ♦ 26
Herb Dip ♦ 25
Horseradish Dip ♦ 20
Hot Pink Dip ♦ 20
Olive-Pecan Spread ♦ 23
Pesto Dip or Spread ♦ 25
Tartar Sauce ♦ 23

Clockwise: Hot Pink Dip (page 20), Celery stuffed with Blue Cheese Spread (page 24), Olive-Pecan Spread on crackers (page 23), Green Dip (page 20)

Green Dip or Spread

Yield: 3½ cups

Enjoy a tasty dip with a rich green color. A good way to get kids to eat spinach. See photo, page 18

Blend in a food processor or blender:
> 2½ cups Mock Sour Cream Dressing, p. 42, omitting the salt.
> 1 lb. fresh spinach, washed, stems removed and chopped (about 4 cups)
> 1 pkg. dried leek soup mix

Per 2 Tbsp. Serving: Calories: 75, Protein: 2 gm., Fat: 5 gm., Carbohydrates: 3 gm.

Horseradish Dip

Yield: 1¼ cups

Blend together in a food processor or blender until smooth and creamy:
> ½ lb. tofu
> 3 Tbsp. oil
> 2 Tbsp. lemon juice
> 2 Tbsp. prepared horseradish
> ½ tsp. salt

Per 2 Tbsp. Serving: Calories: 56, Protein: 2 gm., Fat: 4 gm.,Carbohydrates: 1 gm.

Hot Pink Dip

Yield: 2 Cups

A zippy dip with corn chips. See photo, page 18.

Blend together in a food processor or blender until creamy:
> ½ lb. tofu
> 1-7 ½ oz. can tomatoes and jalapenos
> 1 Tbsp. oil

Per 2 Tbsp. Serving: Calories: 26, Protein: 1 gm, Fat: 1 gm, Carbohydrates: 2 gm.

Far East Dip

Yield: 2 cups

Blend together in a food processor until smooth and creamy:
   ½ lb. tofu
   3 green onions, cut up (3 Tbsp.)
   2 Tbsp. oil
   1 Tbsp. lemon juice
   1 Tbsp. candied ginger, minced

Fold in:
   ¼ cup walnuts, chopped

Per 2 Tbsp. Serving: Calories: 46, Protein: 2 gm., Fat: 3 gm., Carbohydrates: 2 gm.

Cashew Spread

Yield: 1¾ cups

Chop in the food processor:
   ½ cup roasted salted cashews

Reserve ¼ cup to fold in at the end.

Blend in a food processor until smooth and creamy:
   ½ lb. tofu
   2 Tbsp. lemon juice
   2 Tbsp. oil

Fold in the reserved ¼ cup chopped cashews.

Per 2 Tbsp. Serving: Calories: 58, Protein: 2 gm., Fat: 3 gm., Carbohydrates: 2 gm.

Dry Onion Soup Dip

Yield: 2¾ cups

Blend in a food processor or blender until smooth and creamy:
2½ cups Mock Sour Cream Dressing, p. 42, omitting the salt.

Stir or blend in:
1 pkg. dry onion soup mix (scant ½ cup)

Best if refrigerated for about 4 hours or overnight.

Dry Vegetable Soup Dip: Substitute **1 pkg. dried vegetable soup mix** for the dried onion soup mix.

Dry Tomato-Onion Soup Dip: Substitute **1 pkg. dried tomato-onion soup mix** for the dried onion soup mix.

Per ¼ cup serving: Calories: 79, Protein: 2 gm., Fat: 6 gm., Carbohydrates: 3 gm.

Curry-Chutney Dip

Yield: 1¾ cup

Good with raw vegetables or spread on crackers.

Blend together in a food processor or blender until smooth and creamy:
½ lb. tofu
⅓ cup mango chutney
2 Tbsp. oil
1 Tbsp. fresh lemon juice
1 tsp. curry powder
¼ tsp. ground cumin
dash of cayenne (optional)

Per 2 Tbsp. Serving: Calories: 37, Protein: 1 gm., Fat: 2 gm., Carbohydrates: 2 gm.

Olive-Pecan Spread

Yield: 1⅔ cups

This makes a good sandwich spread. Spread on crackers for an appetizer. See photo, page 18.

Blend in a food processor or blender until smooth and creamy.
> **½ lb. tofu**
> **2 Tbsp. oil**
> **3 Tbsp. lemon juice**
> **¼ tsp. salt**

Fold in:
> **¼ cup pecans, cut up**
> **6 Tbsp. pimento olives, sliced**

Per 2 Tbsp. Serving: Calories: 41, Protein: 1 gm., Fat: 1 gm., Carbohydrates: 2 gm.

Tartar Sauce

Yield: 2½ cups

Chop in the food processor:
> **1 small onion (about ½ cup)**

Add:
> **½ lb. tofu**
> **¼ cup lemon juice**
> **2 Tbsp. oil**
> **2 Tbsp. sugar or honey**
> **½ tsp. dry mustard**
> **¾ tsp. salt**

Blend until smooth and creamy, then fold in:
> **¼ cup sweet pickle relish**

Per 2 Tbsp. Serving: Calories: 30, Protein: 1 gm.,Fat: 1 gm., Carbohydrates: 3 gm.

Blue Cheese Spread

Yield: 1¾ cups

Delicious stuffed in celery. See photo, page 18.

Blend in a food processor until smooth and creamy:
- ½ lb. tofu
- 4 oz. blue cheese
- ¼ cup milk or soymilk
- 2 Tbsp. chili sauce
- 2 Tbsp. oil
- 1 Tbsp. vinegar
- ½ tsp. salt
- ¼ tsp. garlic powder
  or one clove garlic, pressed

Per 2 Tbsp. Serving: Calories: 64, Protein: 3 gm., Fat: 4 gm., Carbohydrates: 1 gm.

Cucumber Dill Dip

Yield: 2 cups

Excellent with raw vegetables.

Blend in a food processor or blender until smooth and creamy:
- ½ lb. tofu
- 2 cucumbers, peeled, seeded and cut up
- 8 green onions, chopped
- 4 Tbsp. oil
- 3 Tbsp. white wine
- 2 tsp. dill weed
- ½ tsp. salt
- ⅛ tsp. black pepper

Per 2 Tbsp. Serving: Calories: 44, Protein: 1 gm., Fat: 4 gm., Carbohydrates: 1 gm.

Pesto Dip or Spread

Yield: 1½ cups

Use this spread to make Pesto Pizza, page 78.

Chop in a food processor:
   2 cloves garlic

Add and chop:
   ½ cup fresh basil leaves, packed
   ¼ cup parsley leaves, packed

Add and blend until smooth and creamy:
   ½ lb. tofu
   3 Tbsp. pine nuts or walnuts
   2 Tbsp. Parmesan cheese
   2 Tbsp. olive oil

Per 2 Tbsp. Serving: Calories: 65., Protein: 3 gm., Fat: 2 gm., Carbohydrates: 1 gm.

Herb Dip

Yield: about 1 cup

Blend together in a food processor or blender until smooth and creamy:
   ½ lb. tofu
   2 Tbsp. fresh parsley
   1 Tbsp. olive oil
   ½ tsp. basil
   ½ tsp. oregano
   ½ tsp. salt

Per 2 Tbsp. Serving: Calories: 36, Protein: 2 gm., Fat: 1 gm., Carbohydrates: 1 gm.

Green Goddess Dip

Yield: 1 ½ cups

Chop in the food processor:
1 clove fresh garlic
4 green onions with tops
½ cup parsley leaves

Add and blend together until smooth and creamy:
½ lb. tofu
1 Tbsp. oil
½ tsp. salt
¼ tsp. black pepper
⅛ tsp. tarragon

Per 2 Tbsp. Serving: Calories: 29, Protein: 2 gm., Fat: 1 gm., Carbohydrates: 1 gm.

Avocado Salad ♦ 29
Basil-Garlic Dressing ♦ 41
Chutney Dressing ♦ 41
Cold Curried Rice Salad ♦ 33
Cole Slaw Dressing ♦ 44

Salads and Salad Dressings

Creamy Salad Dressing ♦ 42
Cruise Ship Mustard Dressing ♦ 44
Cucumber-Dill Dressing ♦ 44
Cucumber-Dill Salad ♦ 33
Curry Dressing ♦ 43
Ensalada de Aguacate ♦ 29
Four Bean Salad ♦ 39
Garbanzo Bean Salad ♦ 32
Garlic Lo-Cal Dressing ♦ 43
Iowa Potato Salad ♦ 38
Lebanese Salad for Pita Pockets ♦ 31
Mock Chicken Salad ♦ 32
Mock Sour Cream Dressing ♦ 42
Mom's Fruit Salad Dressing ♦ 42
Pasta-Tofu Salad ♦ 37
Pepper-Pasta Salad ♦ 39
Pineapple-Peanut Slaw ♦ 29
Pink Lo-Cal Dressing ♦ 43
Pinto Bean Salad ♦ 30
Seashell Salad ♦ 37
Sesame Spinach Salad ♦ 40
Spinach-Pine Nut Salad ♦ 30
Stuffed Avocado Salad ♦ 38
Taco Salad ♦ 28
Tofu Salad No.1 ♦ 34
Tofu Salad No.2 ♦ 34
Waldorf Salad ♦ 31

SALADS

Taco Salad

Yield: 4 quarts

Crumble into a bowl:
1 lb. tofu

Sprinkle with:
1-1¾ oz. pkg. taco seasoning mix

Mix this all together and then brown in:
2 Tbsp. oil

While the tofu is browning, mix or arrange the following in a bowl:
2 tomatoes, chopped
1 small head of lettuce, torn in bite size pieces
1 small onion, chopped
1 ripe avocado, cubed
1 cucumber, chopped
½ cup olives, (black or green) chopped

At the last minute before serving, add:
8 oz. corn chips
the flavored tofu

If you toss it all together, serve immediately so the chips won't get soggy, and pass with mild hot sauce for dressing.

Per 2 Cup Serving: Calories: 165, Protein: 6 gm., Fat: 5 gm., Carbohydrates: 8 gm.

Ensalada de Aguacate (Avocado Salad)

Yield: 1½ quarts

See photo, page 35.

Mix together in a blender or shaker jar.
   ¼ cup fresh lime juice
   2 Tbsp. fresh parsley or celantro, chopped
   2 Tbsp. oil
   1 tsp. salt
   1 clove garlic, pressed or ½ tsp. garlic powder
   ¼ tsp. black pepper

Pour this dressing over:
   ¾ lb. tofu, cut in ½" cubes
   2 ripe tomatoes, chopped
   1 ripe avocado, cubed
   1 small sweet green pepper, chopped
   ¼ cup sweet red onion, chopped

Serve on curly or romaine lettuce, in a pita bread with lettuce, or rolled up in a flour tortilla with lettuce.

Per 1 Cup Serving: Calories: 197, Protein: 10 gm., Fat: 6 gm., Carbohydrate: 7 gm.

Pineapple-Peanut Slaw

Yield: 6 cups

Mix together in a bowl:
   3½ cups shredded cabbage
   2 medium carrots, shredded
   14 oz. can pineapple chunks, drained
      or about 2 cups fresh pineapple cut in chunks
   ½ cup roasted unsalted peanuts

Pour over and mix in:
   Cole Slaw Dressing, (1½ cups) p. 44

Per 1 Cup Serving: Calories: 255, Protein: 7 gm., Fat: 11 gm., Carbohydrate: 22 gm.

Spinach-Pine Nut Salad

Yield: 2 quarts

A glass bowl shows off the red and green. See photo on front cover.

Have ready:
> ½ lb. young spinach leaves, washed, stems removed
> 1 small red onion, sliced
> 2 ribs celery, sliced on the diagonal
> ½ cup pine nuts
> ½ lb. tofu, cut in small cubes

Dressing

Shake together in a small jar:
> 2 Tbsp. olive oil
> 2 Tbsp. salad oil
> 2 Tbsp. wine vinegar
> ½ tsp. salt
> ½ tsp. dry mustard
> ¼ tsp. black pepper

Place the tofu cubes in a glass serving bowl. Pour the dressing over and toss to coat. Add the rest and toss to mix well.

Per 1 Cup Serving: Calories: 178, Protein: 9 gm., Fat: 10 gm., Carbohydrates: 7 gm.

Pinto Bean Salad

Yield: 4 cups

Mix together in a salad bowl:
> 1-16 oz. can pinto beans, drained
> 1 lb. tofu, drained, cut in small cubes
> 4 green onions, including tops, chopped
> 8 small radishes, sliced
> ½ cup celery, chopped
> ½ cup bottled Italian salad dressing

Mix all together and serve on red tipped lettuce.

Per ½ Cup Serving: Calories: 149, Protein: 6 gm., Fat: 4 gm., Carbohydrates: 13 gm.

Lebanese Salad for Pita Pockets

Yield: 6 cups

Combine in a jar:
**¼ cup salad oil
2 Tbsp. olive oil
2 Tbsp. lemon juice
½ tsp. salt
1 clove garlic, minced
a few drops hot pepper sauce**

Shake and add to the jar:
1 lb. tofu, cut in small cubes

Toss in a salad bowl:
**2 cups torn lettuce or spinach leaves
1 cup cucumber, seeded and chopped
2 tomatoes, diced
½ cup green onion, chopped
¼ cup currants
¼ cup fresh mint, chopped
¼ cup fresh parsley, chopped**

Stir tofu and dressing into the salad and serve in warm pita breads cut in half.

Per 1 Cup Serving: Calories: 187, Protein: 4 gm., Fat: 10 gm., Carbohydrates: 10 gm.

Waldorf Salad

Yield: 3½ cups

Mix together:
**2 cups apples, chopped
1 Tbsp. lemon juice
1 cup celery, diced
½ cup walnuts, chopped**

Then mix in:
1 cup Mock Sour Cream Dressing, p. 42

Chill and serve.

Per ¾ Cup Serving: Calories: 239, Protein: 6 gm., Fat: 17 gm., Carbohydrates: 14 gm.

Mock Chicken Salad

Yield: 4 cups

Combine in a bowl:
> 1 lb. tofu, cut in ½" cubes
> 2 tbsp. fresh lemon juice
> ½ tsp. celery salt

Mix in:
> 1 cup celery, diced
> ¼ cup green onion, minced
> ½ cup almonds, slivered and toasted
> ½ tsp. salt

Blend together with:
> 1 cup Mock Sour Cream Dressing, p. 42

Chill and serve.

Per 1 Cup Serving: Calories: 336, Protein: 16 gm., Fat: 14 gm., Carbohydrates: 10 gm.

Garbanzo Bean Salad

Yield: 4 cups

For dressing, mix together in a salad bowl:
> ¼ cup oil
> 2 Tbsp. vinegar
> 1 tsp. curry powder
> ½ tsp. salt
> ¼ tsp. black pepper

Add to the mixed dressing:
> 1-20 oz. can garbanzo beans or chick peas, drained
> ½ lb. tofu, grated coarsely
> ½ cup celery, diced
> 2 Tbsp. red onion, minced

Toss and mix, then adjust seasonings. Since curry powders vary in strength, you may want to add more or less. Chill and serve on lettuce.

Per ½ Cup Serving: Calories: 265, Protein: 13 gm., Fat: 7 gm., Carbohydrates: 32 gm.

Cold Curried Rice Salad

Yield: About 2 ½ cups

Have ready:
   1 cup Mock Sour Cream Dressing, p. 42
   1 cup cooked leftover rice

Put the rice in a bowl and mix in:
   ½ cup cucumber, chopped
   ¼ cup green pepper, chopped
   ¼ cup green onion, chopped
   3 Tbsp. mango chutney
   1 Tbsp. lemon juice
   2 tsp. curry powder
   ½ tsp. cumin

Mix in the Mock Sour Cream Dressing, chill and serve on lettuce.

Per ½ Cup Serving: Calories: 170, Protein: 2 gm., Fat: 9 gm., Carbohydrates: 15 gm.

Cucumber-Dill Salad

Yield: about 4 cups

Peel and slice:
   2 medium cucumbers

Sprinkle them with:
   1 tsp. salt
   ice cubes

Put in the refrigerator for about 15 minutes, then rinse, drain, and press out the excess water.

Add:
   1 small onion, chopped
   1¼ cups Mock Sour Cream Dressing, p. 42
   ½ tsp. dill weed

Mix and serve.

Per ½ Cup Serving: Calories: 90, Protein: 3 gm., Fat: 7 gm., Carbohydrates: 2 gm.

Tofu Salad No. 1

Yield: 4 cups

Mix together in a bowl:
  1 lb. tofu, mashed, crumbled or coarsely grated
  ⅓ cup sweet red or yellow pepper, chopped
  ½ cup onion, chopped
  2 Tbsp. fresh parsley, chopped
  1 tsp. dried basil
  1 tsp. garlic powder

Pour over and mix in:
  1¼ cups Creamy Salad Dressing, p. 42 or mayonnaisse

Per ½ Cup Serving: Calories: 129, Protein: 7 gm., Fat: 7 gm., Carbohydrates: 3 gm.

Tofu Salad No. 2

Yield: 4½ cups

See photo, page 35

Mix together in a bowl:
  1 lb. tofu, mashed, crumbled or coarsely grated
  ⅓ cup sweet pickle relish
  ¼ cup onion, chopped or 1 Tbsp. onion powder
  ½ cup celery, chopped
  1 clove garlic, pressed or ¼ tsp. garlic powder
  2 Tbsp. nutritional yeast (optional)
  1 Tbsp. fresh parsley

Pour over and mix in:
  1 recipe Creamy Salad Dressing, p. 42 or mayonnaisse

Per ½ Cup Serving: Calories: 140, Protein: 7 gm., Fat: 7 gm., Carbohydrates: 6 gm.

Clockwise: Ensalada de Aguacate (page 29), Tofu Salad No. 2 in a sandwich (this page), Garlic Lo-Cal Dressing and Pink Lo-Cal Dressing (page 43)

Seashell Salad

Yield: 4½ cups

Cook to *al dente* in boiling salted water:
   1 cup small shell macaroni

Rinse with cold water and drain.

Mix the shells in a bowl with:
   ¾ lb. tofu, cut in small cubes
   1 cup cocktail sauce
   ½ cup celery, chopped
   ½ cup green pepper, chopped
   ¼ cup green onion, chopped
   ¼ cup mayonnaise

Serve on a bed of lettuce.

Per ½ Cup Serving: Calories: 121, Protein: 4 gm., Fat: 3 gm., Carbohydrates: 12 gm.

Pasta-Tofu Salad

Yield: 7 cups

Cook in boiling salted water to *al dente:*
   8 oz. spiral noodles

Rinse with cold water and drain.

Mix together in a salad bowl:
   ½ lb. tofu, grated on the coarse side of a grater
   ½ cup chopped celery
   4 medium green onions with tops, chopped

Toss all together with the noodles.

Mix in:
   2 cups Cruise Ship Mustard Dressing, p. 44

Garnish with:
   1-8 oz. can asparagus tips, drained
      or 1 can artichoke hearts, drained

Per 1 Cup Serving: Calories: 370, Protein: 10 gm., Fat: 11 gm., Carbohydrates: 27 gm.

Corn Chowder (page 47)

Iowa Potato Salad

Yield: 5½ cups

Scrub well and cut up:
   4 medium potatoes

Boil in salted water until tender. Drain and slip skins off, and break or cut into pieces. (If potatoes are well scrubbed, skins can be left on.)

While the potatoes are still hot, toss with a mixture of:
   2 Tbsp. oil   **½ tsp. salt**
   2 Tbsp. vinegar   **⅛ tsp. black pepper**

Let cool. Add to the cooled potatoes:
   ⅓ cup onion, minced   **¼ cup parsley, minced**
   1½ cup celery, diced   **celery salt to taste**

Dressing

Blend in a food processor or blender until smooth and creamy:
   ½ lb. tofu, mashed or crumbled
   3 Tbsp. oil
   3 Tbsp. vinegar
   1 Tbsp. cold water

Mix dressing into salad, chill and serve.

Per ½ Cup Serving: Calories: 105, Protein: 3 gm., Fat: 6 gm., Carbohydrates: 8 gm.

Stuffed Avocado Salad

Yield: 4 servings

Cut in half and remove the seeds from:
   2 avocados

Mix together for filling:
   ½ lb. tofu   **½ tsp. basil**
   ¼ cup pimento, chopped   **½ tsp. salt**
   1 Tbsp. olive oil   **¼ tsp. garlic powder**
   1 Tbsp. red wine vinegar   **¼ tsp. black pepper**

Stuff each avocado half with ½ cup filling.

Per Serving: Calories: 212, Protein: 13 gm., Fat: 4 gm., Carbohydrates: 19 gm.

Pepper-Pasta Salad

Yield: 2 ½ quarts

Cook in boiling salted water to *al dente*:
8 oz. fusilli noodles

Saute together:
2 Tbsp. olive oil
1 sweet green pepper, sliced
2 cloves garlic, minced

Mix all together in a bowl along with:
¾ lb. tofu, grated
½ cup toasted almonds
½ cup prepared Italian salad dressing

Per 1 Cup Serving: Calories: 250, Protein: 8 gm., Fat: 7 gm., Carbohydrates: 23 gm.

Four Bean Salad

Yield: 2 quarts

Blend together in food processor, blender or shaker jar:
½ cup oil
¼ cup cider vinegar
1 tsp. oregano
1 tsp. basil
1 tsp. salt
½ tsp. dry mustard
½ tsp. black pepper

Mix together in a bowl:
½ lb. tofu, cut in small cubes
one small onion, chopped
one rib celery, chopped
one pkg. frozen green beans, cooked

Pour dressing over while green beans are hot, and stir in:
15 oz. can kidney beans, drained and rinsed
15 oz. can garbanzo beans, drained and rinsed

Mix together, and marinate overnight.

Per 1 Cup Serving: Calories: 395, Protein: 17 gm., Fat: 14 gm., Carbohydrates: 45 gm.

Sesame Spinach Salad

Yield: 2 quarts

Have ready:
> ½ lb. spinach leaves, washed
> ½ lb. red tip or leaf lettuce
> ¼ cup red onion, chopped
> ½ lb. tofu, cut in ½" cubes

Mix together for dressing in a jar:
> 2 Tbsp. oil
> 2 Tbsp. white wine vinegar
> 1 Tbsp. soy sauce
> 1 tsp. sesame oil
> ¼ tsp. powdered ginger
> ¼ tsp. garlic powder
> ¼ tsp. black pepper

Heat in a skillet:
> 1 Tbsp. oil

Add and brown while stirring:
> 2 Tbsp. sesame seeds

Add and stir to coat with seeds:
> the tofu cubes

Add the tofu cubes to the pan, mix to coat with seeds, pour dressing into pan, mix, turn off heat. Combine tofu and torn up greens in a 3 quart bowl, tossing gently. Serve immediately.

Garnish with:
> 2 Tbsp. bacon bits (optional) and/or add salt to taste.

Per 1 Cup Serving: Calories: 90, Protein: 4 gm., Fat: 5gm., Carbohydrates: 3gm.

SALAD DRESSINGS

Basil-Garlic Dressing

Yield: 1 ¼ cups

Chop in a food processor:
  4 cloves garlic

Add and chop:
  ½ cup fresh basil leaves, packed

Add and blend until smooth and creamy:
  ½ lb. tofu
  2 Tbsp. olive oil
  2 Tbsp. salad oil
  2 Tbsp. red wine vinegar
  ½ tsp. salt

Per 2 Tbsp. Serving: Calories: 66, Protein: 2 gm., Fat: 3 gm., Carbohydrates: 1 gm.

Chutney Dressing

Yield: 1 ¾ cups

Blend together in a food processor or blender until smooth and creamy:
  ½ lb. tofu
  3 Tbsp. chutney
  2 Tbsp. oil
  1 Tbsp. lemon juice
  ½ tsp. salt
  ¼ cup water

Per 2 Tbsp. Serving: Calories: 32, Protein: 1 gm., Fat: 2 gm., Carbohydrates: 1 gm.

Mock Sour Cream Dressing

Yield: 1¼ cups

This low calorie, no cholesterol dressing can be used in a variety of recipes that call for sour cream.

Blend in a food processor or blender until smooth and creamy:
- ½ lb. tofu
- ¼ cup oil
- 2 Tbsp. lemon juice
- 1 ½ tsp. honey or sugar (optional)
- ½ tsp. salt

Per 2 Tbsp. Serving: Calories: 67, Protein: 2 gm., Fat: 6 gm., Carbohydrates: 1 gm.

Mom's Fruit Salad Dressing

Yield: 2 ½ cups

Blend together in a food processor or blender until smooth and creamy:

1 cup oil	2 Tbsp. celery seed
¼ lb. tofu	1½ tsp. dry mustard
½ cup honey	1 ¼ tsp. salt
½ cup vinegar	1 tsp. paprika
2 Tbsp. onion, minced	

Per 2 Tbsp. Serving: Calories: 130, Protein: 1 gm., Fat: 11 gm., Carbohydrates: 7 gm.

Creamy Salad Dressing

Yield: 1¼ cups

A low calorie, no cholesterol substitute for mayonnaise.

Blend together in a food processor or blender until smooth and creamy:

½ lb. soft tofu	1 tsp. Dijon mustard (optional)
¼ cup oil	½ tsp. salt
3 Tbsp. cider vinegar	¼ tsp. black pepper
1 Tbsp. sugar or honey	

Per 2 Tbsp. Serving: Calories: 67, Protein: 2 gm., Fat: 5 gm.,Carbohydrates: 1 gm.

Curry Dressing

Yield: 1 cup

A dressing for fruit salad.

Blend in a food processor or blender until smooth and creamy:
   ¼ lb. tofu
   ¼ cup oil
   3 Tbsp. lemon juice
   1 Tbsp. honey
   ½ tsp. curry
   ¼ tsp. ginger
   ¼ tsp. salt

Per 2 Tbsp. Serving: Calories: 82, Protein: 1 gm., Fat: 7 gm., Carbohydrates: 3 gm.

Garlic Lo-Cal Dressing

Yield: 1¼ cups

See photo, page 35.

Chop in a food processor:
   2 cloves garlic

Add and blend until smooth and creamy:
   ½ lb. tofu
   ¼ cup white vinegar
   2 Tbsp. oil
   2 Tbsp. water - if needed
   ½ tsp. salt
   ¼ tsp. dry mustard
   ¼ tsp. black pepper

Per 2 Tbsp. Serving: Calories: 42, Protein: 2 gm., Fat: 3 gm., Carbohydrates: 1 gm.

Pink Lo-Cal Dressing: Blend in **¼ cup ketchup** with the rest of the ingredients.

Cole Slaw Dressing

Yield: 1½ cups

Blend together in a food processor or blender until smooth and creamy:
½ lb. tofu
¼ cup oil
¼ cup cider vinegar
¼ cup sugar or 2 Tbsp. honey
¼ tsp. salt
¼ tsp. black pepper
½ small onion

This is enough to dress 4 cups shredded vegetables.

Per 2 Tbsp. Serving: Calories: 73, Protein: 2 gm., Fat 5 gm., Carbohydrates: 5 gm.

Cucumber-Dill Dressing

Yield: 2 ½ cups

Blend in a food processor or blender until smooth and creamy:
½ lb. tofu
1 medium cucumber, peeled and cut in 8 pieces
2 Tbsp. white rice vinegar
2 Tbsp. oil
½ tsp. salt
¼ tsp. black pepper

Per 2 Tbsp. Serving: Calories: 22, Protein: 1 gm., Fat: 1 gm., Carbohydrates: 1 gm.

Cruise Ship Mustard Dressing

Yield: 1 cup

Combine in a food processor or blender:
¼ lb. tofu
2 Tbsp. Dijon mustard
2 Tbsp. lemon juice
1 Tbsp. Parmesan cheese
¼ tsp. salt

Add while processing:
⅓ cup salad oil

Per 2 Tbsp. Serving: Calories: 66, Protein: 1 gm., Fat: 6 gm., Carbohydrates: 5 gm.

Soups

Chunky Gazpacho ◆ 50
Corn Chowder ◆ 47
Gumbo Soup ◆ 46
Lentil Soup ◆ 52
Miso Vegetable Soup ◆ 49
Mock Vichysoisse ◆ 52
Potato Tofu Soup ◆ 52
Pumpkin Soup ◆ 51
Quick Vegetable Tofu Soup ◆ 46
Ramen Noodle Soup ◆ 48
Southwestern Chili ◆ 48
Spinach Soup ◆ 50

Gumbo Soup

Yield: 6 cups

Have ready:
½ lb. frozen tofu, thawed, squeezed out and chopped.

Bubble together in a heavy bottom soup pan until the color of peanut butter:
2 Tbsp. oil
2 Tbsp. flour

Stir in:
2 cups water
3 tsp. vegetable boullion

Bring to a boil and add:
1 lb. frozen vegetable gumbo mixture
the tofu
1-15 oz. can peeled tomatoes, chopped with juice
1 bay leaf

Stir, cover and bring to a boil. Let simmer 18-20 minutes until the vegetables are tender. Serve along with hot cooked rice.

Per 1 Cup Serving: Calories: 157, Protein: 7 gm., Fat: 5 gm., Carbohydrates: 19 gm.

Quick Vegetable Tofu Soup

Yield: 4 cups

Bring to a boil in a small saucepan:
4½ cups water

Add:
¼ lb. tofu, cut in small cubes

When water boils again, stir in with a wire wisk:
1-1.4 oz. pkg. dry vegetable soup mix

Reduce heat to low and simmer 20 minutes.

Per 1 Cup Serving: Calories: 93, Protein: 4 gm., Fat: 1 gm., Carbohydrates: 13 gm.

Corn Chowder

Yield: 2 quarts

See photo, page 36.

Have ready:
>2 onions, chopped
>1 bell pepper (red or green), chopped
>2 ribs celery, chopped
>2 small potatoes, cut in ½" cubes
>2 cloves garlic, pressed

Heat in a sauce pan:
>2 Tbsp. oil

Add all the chopped vegetables, stir and cook until onions are transparent.

Then add:
>4 cups water
>1 small bay leaf
>¼ tsp. thyme

When it comes to a boil and the vegetables are almost tender, add:
>4 tsp. vegetable boullion
>2½ cups frozen corn
>½ lb. tofu, cut in ¼" cubes
>¼ tsp. freshly ground black pepper

Serve when corn is tender. Garnish with red and green bell pepper rings.

Per 1 Cup Serving: Calories: 131, Protein: 5 gm., Fat: 4 gm., Carbohydrates: 18 gm.

Southwestern Chili

Yield: 7 cups

Have ready:
    1 lb. frozen tofu, thawed, squeezed dry
    and torn into bite-size pieces

Saute in a 2½ to 3 quart soup pot:
    2 Tbsp. oil
    1 medium green pepper, diced
    1 medium onion, diced
    2 cloves garlic, minced

When they are almost tender, add:
    the tofu pieces
    1½ Tbsp. chili powder
    1 tsp. cumin
    1 tsp. salt

Saute all together until vegetables are tender, then add:
    1-30 oz. can pinto or kidney beans
    3 cups water

Heat until hot and serve.

Per 1 Cup Serving: Calories: 221, Protein: 14 gm., Fat: 4 gm., Carbohydrates: 27 gm.

Ramen Noodle Soup

Yield: 2½ cups per pkg.

Packaged ramen noodle soups are available in a number of different brand names. They contain ready to cook noodles and a prepared flavoring mixture. With your added tofu and vegetables, this becomes a quick and easy lunch, snack or light supper. Start by preparing any vegetables you'd like to have in the soup, or whatever you have on hand: carrots, onion, broccoli, cabbage, greens, parsley, and so on. Slice everything very thin so it will cook quickly. If you have leftover cooked vegetables, save them to add last.

Have ready:
    ½ cup raw vegetables per serving, sliced thin
    ½ oz. tofu per serving, cut into ½" cubes or strips
    (this tofu can be either fresh or frozen.)

Bring the water called for on the package to a boil. Add the thinly sliced vegetables, noodles and tofu. When the noodles are done, turn off the heat and add the flavoring and any leftover vegetables you want to add. Serve garnished with chopped green onion.

Per 1 Cup Serving: Calories: 200, Protein: 8 gm., Fat: 1 gm., Carbohydrates: 28 gm.

Miso Vegetable Soup

Yield: 10 cups

Made from scratch, but parboiling carrots shortens cooking time.

Have ready:
1 cup carrots, sliced   **1 cup celery, sliced**
1 cup onions, sliced   **4 cups napa or cabbage, shredded**

Heat in a 6 qt. soup kettle:
¼ cup oil

Add the onions, saute a few minutes, then add celery and cabbage and stir fry over meduim heat.

While the other vegetables are cooking, parboil the carrots 2 minutes in:
1 cup boiling water

Add carrots and cooking water to the soup pot along with:
2 Tbsp. vegetable boullion granules
5 cups boiling water
¼ tsp. black pepper
¼ tsp. garlic powder

Bring to a boil, reduce heat and simmer 5 minutes.

Stir in:
1 lb. tofu, cut ½" cubes

Make a paste of:
3 Tbsp. miso
½ cup cold water

Stir this into the soup at the very last and do not boil afterward.

Per 1 Cup Serving: Calories: 107, Protein: 5 gm., Fat: 6 gm., Carbohydrates: 6 gm.

Chunky Gazpacho

Yield: 6 cups

Mix together in a bowl:
- **3 cups fresh tomatoes, peeled and chopped**
- **½ lb. tofu, cut in small cubes**
- **2 cups tomato juice**
- **1 medium cucumber, seeded and chopped**
  (about 1 ¼ cup)
- **⅓ cup green pepper, minced**
- **¼ cup green onion, minced**
- **1½ Tbsp. fresh parsley, minced**
- **1 Tbsp. olive oil**
- **1 Tbsp. red wine vinegar**
- **1 tsp. salt**
- **¼ tsp. garlic powder**
- **¼ tsp. basil**
- **¼ tsp. oregano**
- **⅛ tsp. black pepper**

Chill and serve.

Per 1 Cup Serving: Calories: 86, Protein: 5 gm., Fat: 1 gm., Carbohydrates: 9 gm.

Spinach Soup

Yield: 4 cups

Have ready:
- **1-10 oz. pkg. frozen spinach, thawed and drained**
- **3 cups vegetable boullion**
- **½ cup instant mashed potato flakes**

Saute together:
- **2 Tbsp. margarine**
- **2 Tbsp. onion, chopped**

Remove from heat and crumble in:
- **½ lb. tofu**

Pour the vegetable boullion over the spinach in a saucepan and heat.

Stir together:
- **½ cup milk**
- **½ cup of the vegetable broth**

Pour this over the instant mashed potato flakes and fluff with a fork. Stir this together with the rest of the boullion and spinach.

Process half at a time in the food processor along with:
    ½ cup milk or soymilk if necessary to thin

Return to the kettle. Serve hot, but do not boil.

Per 1 Cup Serving: Calories: 210, Protein: 8 gm., Fat: 4 gm., Carbohydrates: 29 gm.

Pumpkin Soup

Yield: 7 cups

Saute in a 2½ quart soup pot:
    2 Tbsp. oil
    2 cups potatoes, cut in cubes
    1 medium onion, chopped
    3 cloves garlic, minced

When almost done, add:
    ½ lb. tofu, cut in cubes

Sprinkle well with:
    1½ tsp. salt
    ½ tsp. black pepper

When the potatoes are soft, stir in:
    1-16 oz. can pumpkin
    3 cups water

Heat until hot and serve.

Per 1 Cup Serving: Calories: 126, Protein: 5 gm., Fat: 4 gm., Carbohydrates: 15 gm.

Potato Tofu Soup

Yield: 2 quarts

Cook together in a kettle until tender (about 20 minutes):
4 cups boiling water
4 medium potatoes, peeled and cut up (4 cups)
1 medium onion, chopped
½ tsp. salt

While they are cooking, blend in a food processor until creamy:
½ lb. tofu
2 Tbsp. oil

When potatoes and onions are done remove from the pot with a slotted spoon and add to the processor.

Blend tofu and potatoes until creamy, then pour back into the potato water and stir in:
¼ tsp. black pepper

Adjust the seasonings and heat. If the soup is too thick, add:
½ cup milk or soymilk

To serve, put 1 pat margarine or butter in each bowl, then ladle in soup.
Sprinkle with chopped parsley.

Per 1 Cup Serving: Calories: 100, Protein: 3 gm., Fat: 4 gm., Carbohydrates: 10 gm.

Mock Vichysoisse: Serve the soup cold, sprinkled with minced chives.

Lentil Soup

Yield: 3 cups

Add tofu to already prepared soups for extra protein.

Heat together:
1-19 oz. can lentil soup
⅓ lb. tofu, cut in small cubes

Per 1 Cup Serving: Calories: 214, Protein: 17 gm., Fat: 1 gm., Carbohydrates: 33 gm.

Tofu Tacos and Tostadas (page 75)

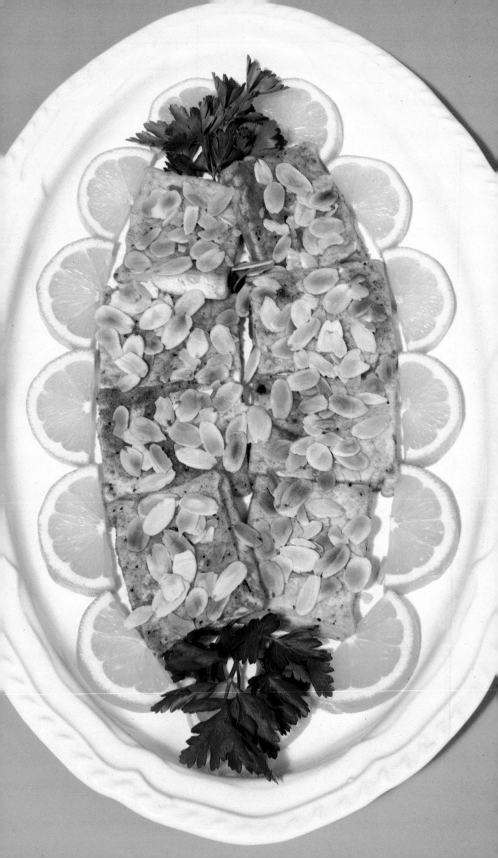

Amandine Tofu ◆ 61
Angel Hair Primavera ◆ 74
Barbecue Tofu ◆ 57
Broccoli-Mushroom Stir Fry ◆ 64
Burritos Fritos ◆ 80

Main Dishes

Cabbage Tofu Stir Fry ◆ 62
Chile Quiles ◆ 64
Chinese Fried Rice with Tofu ◆ 76
Curry ◆ 76
Deviled Tofu ◆ 77
Enchilada Casserole ◆ 65
Golden Rice ◆ 80
Green Rice ◆ 60
Hawaiian Stir Fry ◆ 70
Lasagne ◆ 66
Lasagne Florentine ◆ 66
Lasagne with Cheese ◆ 67
Macaroni and Tofu and Cheese ◆ 60
Noodles Romanoff ◆ 73
Orange Tofu ◆ 59
Oriental Stir Fry ◆ 74
Oven Fried Tofu ◆ 58
Pesto Pizza ◆ 78
Pizza Burritos ◆ 79
Pizza with Tofu ◆ 78
Quick and Easy Fried Tofu ◆ 56
Sloppy Joes ◆ 81
Spinach Triangles ◆ 82
Spring Rolls ◆ 68
Stroganoff ◆ 63
Stuffed Jumbo Shells ◆ 62
Tamale Pie ◆ 69
Tofu Burgers ◆ 56
Tofu Loaf ◆ 57
Tofu Spaghetti Balls ◆ 57
Tofu Tacos ◆ 75
Tostadas ◆ 75

Amandine Tofu (page 61)

Quick and Easy Fried Tofu

Yield: 8 slices

Perhaps the quickest and easiest way to serve tofu hot for a meal or snack is to pan fry it. The flavor it takes on depends on what flavoring is added to it either before or while it is cooking.

Cut into 8 slices:
   1 lb. tofu

Pour in a shallow dish:
   2 tsp. soy sauce

Dip each slice in the soy sauce and then brown on each side in:
   2 Tbsp. oil

While it is cooking, sprinkle with any of the following to taste:

garlic powder	**oregano**
onion powder	**poultry seasoning**
basil	**curry powder**

Serve with noodles, rice, millet, buckwheat groats, potatoes or in sandwiches.

Instead of dipping the slices in soy sauce, try spreading each slice with a thin layer of **Vegemite™, Marmite™ or miso** before frying.

The tofu can be cut in cubes or crumbled instead of sliced.

Per Slice: Calories: 74, Protein: 5 gm., Fat: 4 gm., Carbohydrates: 2 gm.

Breaded & Fried Tofu: After dipping the tofu slices in soy sauce, dredge in any of the breadings listed for Oven Fried Tofu, page 58-59, and then pan fry.

Tofu Burgers

Yield: 8 burgers

Mix together in bowl:
   1 lb. tofu, mashed or crumbled

½ cup oatmeal	**1 tsp. salt**
½ cup wheat germ	**1 tsp. poultry seasoning**
2 Tbsp. onion powder	**or ½ tsp. basil and ½ tsp. oregano**
1½ Tbsp. parsley, chopped	**½ tsp. garlic powder**

Shape into 8 burgers and brown in:
   2 Tbsp. oil

Serve on buns with all the fixings.

Per Burger: Calories: 118, Protein: 7 gm., Fat: 4 gm., Carbohydrates: 8 gm.

Tofu Spaghetti Balls: Shape the mix into 20 balls and carefully brown in ½ cup oil.

Tofu Loaf: Press the mix above into an oiled loaf pan, top with ¼ cup ketchup and bake at 350° F. for about 30 minutes. Let it cool for about 10 minutes before slicing. This makes good sandwiches cold or refried.

Barbecue Tofu

Yield: 12 ribs or 8 slices

These ribs can be served as a main dish or cut smaller for an appetizer.

Preheat oven or toaster oven to 400° F.

Have ready:
   1 lb. frozen tofu, thawed, squeezed dry and cut into rib-like strips
      or 1 lb. fresh tofu cut in 8 slices
   ¾ cup your favorite barbecue sauce

Oil a 9″ by 13″ pan (smaller for a toaster oven) with:
   2 Tbsp. oil

Lay the pieces of tofu in the pan, leaving space between each one. Bake for 10 to 15 minutes or until browned on one side, then turn over and bake about 5-10 minutes to brown the other side. Pour and spread the barbecue sauce over all the pieces and bake 5-10 more minutes. Cooking can also be done on an outdoor grill. Serve on Kaiser rolls or with rice or potatoes. Barbecue Tofu can be frozen and reheated later.

Per Rib: Calories: 65, Protein: 3 gm., Fat: 2 gm., Carbohydrates: 5 gm.

Oven Fried Tofu

Yield: 8 slices

Keep one or more of these breadings for baked tofu on hand in a covered container for quick preparation.

Preheat oven to 375° F.

Cut into 8 slices:
1 lb. firm tofu

Mix together in a bowl for breading:
⅓ cup flour or bread crumbs
2 Tbsp. nutritional yeast
1 Tbsp. onion powder
¼ tsp. poultry seasoning
⅛ tsp. garlic powder

Pour into a flat bowl:
2 tsp. soy sauce

Spread a cookie sheet with:
2 Tbsp. oil

Dip each slice of tofu into the soy sauce on both sides and then dredge in flour mixture using the one hand wet and one hand dry method. Arrange breaded slices on the oiled cookie sheet. Bake 15 minutes on one side, then about 10 minutes on the other, or until both sides are browned. Add more oil to the pan if needed when you flip the pieces. Serve like "cutlets" or in sandwiches.

Per Serving: Calories: 89, Protein: 5 gm., Fat: 4 gm., Carbohydrates: 5 gm.

Breading No. 2
Mix together:
¼ cup flour or bread crumbs
1 pkg. dry onion-mushroom soup mix

Breading No. 3
Mix together:
2 Tbsp. bread crumbs
1 pkg. dry tomato-onion soup mix

Breading No. 4

Mix together:
- ⅓ cup flour or breadcrumbs
- 1 Tbsp. onion powder
- 1 tsp. chili powder
- 1 tsp. parsley flakes
- ¼ tsp. garlic powder

Breading No. 5

Mix together:
- ⅓ cup flour
- 1 Tbsp. onion powder
- ½ tsp. basil
- ¼ tsp. garlic powder

Orange Tofu

Yield: 4 Servings

Cut into 8 slices:
- 1 lb. tofu

Mix together:
- ⅔ cup flour
- 1 tsp. paprika
- 1 tsp. thyme
- 1 tsp. salt
- ¼ tsp. black pepper

Dredge the tofu slices in the flour mixture, then lightly brown on each side in:
- 2 Tbsp. oil

While tofu is cooking, mix together:
- 1 cup juice from 1-2 navel oranges
- 2 tsp. grated rind from the oranges

Remove the tofu slices to a serving platter and pour the juice mixture over.

Fresh orange slices make a nice garnish.

Per Slice: Calories: 121, Protein: 6 gm., Fat: 4 gm., Carbohydrates: 12 gm.

Macaroni and Tofu and Cheese

Yield: 5 cups

Extra added protein for a quick meal.

Have ready:
1-7 ¼ oz. pkg. macaroni and cheese

Boil the macaroni until *al dente* in:
6 cups boiling water
1 tsp. salt

Melt in a saucepan:
¼ cup margarine

Stir in:
½ cup milk or soymilk
the packaged cheese mix
½ lb. tofu, crumbled

Heat and stir until hot, then add the drained macaroni.

Per 1 Cup Serving: Calories: 408, Protein: 19 gm., Fat: 19 gm., Carbohydrates: 36 gm.

Green Rice

Yield: 3 cups

Preheat oven to 375° F.

Have ready:
2 cups cooked rice
1 pkg. frozen chopped spinach, thawed and drained

Blend in a food processor or blender:
½ lb. tofu
2 Tbsp. oil
2 Tbsp. vinegar
½ tsp. salt

Saute in a small pan:
1 medium onion, chopped
2 Tbsp. oil

Add everything to the tofu mixture and mix together along with:
   ½ cup sliced almonds
   ½ tsp. garlic powder
   ¼ tsp. nutmeg
   ¼ tsp. black pepper

Bake in an oiled quart baking dish for about 25 minutes.

Per ½ cup Serving: Calories: 278, Protein: 9 gm., Fat: 10 gm., Carbohydrates: 24 gm.

Amandine Tofu

Yield: 4 servings

See photo, page 54.

Cut into 8 slices:
   ½ lb. tofu

Mix together:
   ⅓ cup flour
   1 tsp. paprika
   1 tsp. salt
   ¼ tsp. black pepper

Dredge the tofu slices in the flour mixture, then brown on both sides in:
   2 Tbsp. oil

Remove to a warm serving plate and sprinkle with:
   juice of ½ fresh lemon

Cover with:
   ½ cup toasted slivered almonds

Per Slice: Calories: 122, Protein: 4 gm., Fat: 5 gm., Carbohydrates: 6 gm.

Stuffed Jumbo Shells

Yield: 10 shells

See photo on front cover.

Have ready:
3 cups your favorite tomato sauce

Boil in salted water to *al dente*:
4 oz. jumbo macaroni shells

Mix together:
**1 ½ lbs. tofu mashed
  or 1 lb. tofu, mashed, and ½ lb. mozzarella,
  Munster or Jack cheese, grated
¼ cup fresh parsley, chopped
2 Tbsp. onion powder
1 ½ tsp. salt
½ tsp. garlic powder
½ tsp. basil**

Spread 2 cups tomato sauce on the bottom of a 9" x 9" pan. Spoon the tofu mixture into the cooked shells, about ⅓ cup per shell. and arrange in the pan. Add ½ cup water to the remaining sauce, then pour stripes of sauce over the top of the shells. Top with optional Parmesan cheese. Bake at 350° F. until the tomato sauce is bubbly, about 25 minutes.

Per Shell: Calories: 117, Protein: 8 gm. Fat: 0 gm., Carbohydrates: 16 gm.

Cabbage Tofu Stir Fry

Yield: 6 cups

Have ready:
**6 cups savoy or chinese cabbage, shredded
2 Tbsp. sesame seeds
1 tsp. ginger root, chopped
1 lb. tofu, cut into ¾" cubes**

Mix together and set aside:
**2 Tbsp. white wine vinegar
2 Tbsp. soy sauce
1 Tbsp. sesame oil
2 tsp. corn starch
1 tsp. sugar or honey**

Heat in a wok:
2 Tbsp. oil

Add the sesame seeds and ginger root and stir fry for one minute. Add the cabbage and stir fry 2-3 minutes. Add the tofu and stir fry 1 more minute. Pour in the sauce and cook one minute more, stirring to coat. Serve with rice or noodles.

Per 1 Cup Serving: Calories: 147, Protein: 9 gm., Fat: 6 gm., Carbohydrates: 7 gm.

Stroganoff

Yield: 4 cups

Have ready:
**1 lb. frozen tofu, thawed, squeezed out
and torn in bite size pieces**

Saute together:
**2 Tbsp. oil
1 large onion, chopped
6 oz. mushrooms, sliced
1 large clove garlic, minced**

When the onions are almost transparent, add:
the tofu pieces

Stir and fry until tofu starts to brown. Then stir in:
**1-10 ¾ oz. can cream of mushroom soup
1 can water**

Serve hot on rice or noodles.

Per 1 Cup Serving: Calories: 264, Protein: 12 gm., Fat: 12 gm., Carbohydrates: 14 gm.

Broccoli-Mushroom Stir Fry

Yield: 4 servings

Have ready:
   flowerettes off 1 ½ lbs. broccoli
   1 cup mushrooms, sliced
   ½ lb. tofu, cut in small cubes
   ½ cup walnuts, coarsely chopped
   1 Tbsp. fresh ginger root, minced
   2 Tbsp. soy sauce

Heat in a wok:
   2 Tbsp. oil
   1 tsp. sesame oil

Add ginger root and stir fry one minute. Add mushrooms and stir fry three minutes. Add broccoli and stir fry for about 6 minutes, then cover and steam until they are crisp-tender. Stir in the tofu, soy sauce and walnuts; cook one more minute. Serve at once on rice or chinese noodles.

Per Serving: Calories: 250, Protein: 12 gm., Fat: 21 gm., Carbohydrates: 10 gm.

Chile Quiles

Yield: 4 servings

Serve with a green salad for a quick lunch or dinner.

Mix together:
   1 lb. tofu, mashed
   1 cup picante sauce, your choice how hot
   1 tsp. salt

Cut into quarters:
   12 corn tortillas

Stir fry the cut tortillas in a wok with:
   2 Tbsp. oil

Stir fry until the tortillas start to get crisp, then mix in the tofu mixture and continue to stir fry until all is heated through. Serve.

Per Serving: Calories: 368, Protein: 15 gm., Fat: 5 gm,. Carbohydrates: 47 gm.

Enchilada Casserole

Yield: 4 servings

Preheat oven to 350° F.

Thaw, squeeze and tear into bite-size pieces:
1 lb. frozen tofu (you can substitute fresh tofu)

Have ready:
12 masa (corn) tortillas

Prepare chili gravy, below:

Saute until soft:
2 Tbsp. oil
½ large onion, chopped fine

Mix together in a separate bowl:
3 Tbsp. chili powder
3 Tbsp. unbleached white flour
½ tsp. garlic powder
½ tsp. cumin
1 tsp. salt

Add this to the soft onion, then whip in slowly without making lumps:
4 cups water

Bring to a boil.

Cover the bottom of an 9" x 9" pan with chili gravy. Lay half the tortillas, overlapping evenly. Cover with the tofu pieces, then more tortillas and the rest of the chili gravy.

Sprinkle with:
½ cup Monterey Jack cheese, grated
½ cup black olives, chopped

Bake until bubbling, about 20-25 minutes.

Per Serving: Calories: 504, Protein: 20 gm., Fat: 18 gm., Carbohydrates: 48 gm.

Lasagne

Yield: 4 servings

Preheat oven to 350° F.

Cook in boiling water to *al dente*, then drain and rinse:
½ lb. lasagne noodles

Have ready:
4 cups your favorite tomato sauce

Saute together:
2 Tbsp. oil
1 medium onion, chopped fine

Blend in a food processor or blender until smooth and creamy:
1 lb. tofu, mashed or crumbled
¼ cup oil
1 tsp.salt
¼ tsp. garlic powder

Mix in the sauted onions and:
½ cup fresh parsley, chopped fine

Start making layers in a 2 quart baking dish, beginning with half the tomato sauce on the bottom, then a layer of half the noodles, next the tofu filling, the other half of the noodles, and the rest of the tomato sauce.

This can be topped with:
½ cup grated mozzarella or Parmesan cheese (optional)

Bake for about 30 minutes or until bubbling and cheese is melted.

Per Serving: Calories: 625, Protein: 22 gm., Fat: 24 gm., Carbohydrates: 74 gm.

Lasagne Florentine

Yield: 4 servings

Preheat oven to 350° F.

Cook in boiling water to *al dente*, then drain and rinse:
½ lb. lasagne noodles

Have ready:
4 cups your favorite tomato sauce

Mix together:
1 lb. tofu, mashed or crumbled
1-10 oz. pkg. frozen chopped spinach, thawed
   or 1 lb. fresh spinach, washed and chopped
1 Tbsp. onion powder
1 tsp. salt
½ tsp. garlic powder
½ tsp. basil

Start making layers in a 2 quart baking dish, beginning with half the tomato sauce on the bottom, then a layer of half the noodles, next the tofu filling, the other half of the noodles, and the rest of the tomato sauce. Top with **optional Parmesan or mozzarella cheese.**

Bake for about 30 minutes or until bubbly.

Per Serving: Calories: 368, Protein: 15 gm., Fat: 2 gm., Carbohydrates: 72 gm.

Lasagne with Cheese

Yield: 4 servings

Preheat oven to 350° F.

Cook in boiling water to *al dente*, then rinse and drain:
½ lb. lasagne noodles

Have ready:
4 cups your favorite tomato sauce

Mix together:
1 lb. tofu, mashed   **1 Tbsp. onion powder**
6 oz. grated mozzarella   **1 tsp. salt**
¼ cup fresh parsley, chopped **¼ tsp. garlic powder**

Start making layers in a 2 quart baking dish, beginning with half the tomato sauce on the bottom, then a layer of half the noodles, next the tofu filling, the other half of the noodles, and the rest of the tomato sauce. Top with **optional Parmesan cheese.**

Bake for about 30 minutes or until bubbly.

Per Serving: Calories: 551, Protein: 30 gm., Fat: 9 gm., Carbohydrates: 73 gm.

Spring Rolls

Have all ingredients cut and ready before starting.

Cut into small pieces (1″ x ½″ x ¼″):
  ½ lb. tofu

Sprinkle over with:
  1 Tbsp. soy sauce

Set aside. In a wok or frying pan begin stir frying:
  2 Tbsp. oil
  1 clove garlic, pressed
  1 ½ Tbsp. ginger root, peeled and minced

Add and continue stir frying for one minute:
  2 green onions, cut in 1″ pieces
  1 cup fresh mushrooms, sliced
Add:
  2 cups greens, chopped
    (bok choy, chinese cabbage, or other greens)
  1-4 oz. can water chestnuts, drained and sliced
  the tofu pieces

Stir, cover and steam for 2 minutes, then add:
  2 cups fresh mung bean sprouts

Stir in, then spoon about ⅓ cup into each ready-made spring roll wrapper. Fold up and seal the edges with a dab of water on your finger. Fry in hot oil on both sides until browned. Spring rolls can also be oven fried by placing the rolls on a well oiled cookie sheet and brushing the tops with oil. Bake in a 400° F. oven 10-15 minutes on each side.

Per Spring Roll: Calories: 143, Protein: 5 gm., Fat: 7 gm., Carbohydrates: 14 gm.

Tamale Pie

Yield: 6 servings

Preheat oven to 350° F.

Have ready:
> **1 lb. frozen tofu, thawed, squeezed out
> and torn into bite size pieces**

Saute until transparent:
> **2 Tbsp. oil
> 1 medium green pepper, chopped
> 1 medium onion, chopped
> 2 cloves garlic, minced**

When almost tender add:
> **the tofu pieces
> 2 Tbsp. chili powder
> ½ tsp. cumin
> ½ tsp. salt
> ¼ tsp. oregano**

Stir and fry for a few minutes, then add:
> **1-16 oz. can whole tomatoes, chopped
> 1-15 oz. can tomato sauce
> 1-10 oz. pkg. frozen cut corn
> 1-6 oz. can green chilies, chopped
> ½ cup whole small pitted black olives, drained**

Mix well and pour into a 2 ½ quart casserole or a 9″ X 13″ pan. Cover the top with cornbread topping made from:
> **2-8 oz. pkgs. corn muffin mix**

Bake for about 25 minutes or until cornbread is browned.

Per Serving: Calories: 551, Protein: 16 gm., Fat: 14 gm., Carbohydrates: 79 gm.

Hawaiian Stir Fry

Yield: 6 servings

See photo, page 71.

Having everything ready on a tray before heating the wok or skillet makes stir frying easy.

Have ready:
   1 lb. tofu, cut in ¾" cubes and sprinkled with 3 Tbsp. soy sauce
   1-5 oz. can water chestnuts, sliced and drained
   1-15 oz. can unsweetened pineapple chunks, drained, reserving juice
   1 green pepper, cut in 1" triangles
   1 sweet red pepper, cut in 1" triangles
   1 medium onion, cut in wedges

Stir together in a small saucepan:
   ¼ cup vinegar
   2 Tbsp. cornstarch

Stir in:
   ¼ cup honey
   ½ cup vegetable stock
   the reserved pineapple juice

Cook and whisk over medium heat until clear and bubbly. Set aside.

Heat in a wok or skillet:
   3 Tbsp. oil

Stir in:
   1 tsp. ginger root, minced

Stir in the onion wedges, cook for 2 minutes, add tofu, cook for 1 minute. Add peppers and pineapple, stir. Add chestnuts and sauce. Serve on rice with Chinese noodles.

Per Serving: Calories: 265, Protein: 8 gm., Fat: 7 gm., Carbohydrates: 39 gm.

Hawaiian Stir Fry (this page)

Noodles Romanoff

Yield: 8 cups

Preheat oven to 350° F.

Boil in salted water until *al dente:*
1 lb. flat narrow noodles

Melt in a small saucepan:
½ cup margarine or butter

While it is melting, add to soften:
1 medium onion, chopped
2 cloves garlic, minced

Blend in a food processor or blender until smooth and creamy:
½ lb. tofu
½ cup milk or soymilk

Combine onions, tofu and the cooked, drained noodles

Stir in:
½ cup fresh parsley, chopped
⅓ cup Parmesan cheese

Pour into a 10 cup baking dish and bake for 15 minutes. Serve with more Parmesan cheese. This can be made ahead and reheated later. It is also ready to eat without the baking, if you are in a big rush.

Per 1 Cup Serving: Calories: 231, Protein: 7 gm., Fat: 6 gm., Carbohydrates: 17 gm.

Clockwise: Creamy Cookie Pudding (page 88), Apricot Pudding (page 88) and Raspberry Pudding (page 89)

Oriental Stir Fry

Yield: 5 cups

Have ready:
   1 large onion, sliced
   2 ribs celery, sliced
   ¼ lb. snow pea pods, trimmed
   ¼ lb. fresh bean sprouts
   1-8 oz. can sliced water chestnuts, drained
   1-6 oz. can sliced mushrooms
      or 1 cup fresh mushrooms
   6 small green onions, sliced with tops
   ½ lb. tofu cut in ¾" cubes

Heat in a wok or skillet:
   2 Tbsp. oil

Add the sliced onion and stir fry two minutes. Add snow peas and fresh mushrooms if you are using them and stir fry for another 2 minutes. Stir in water chestnuts, canned mushrooms if you are using them, sprouts and green onions.

Next stir in the tofu and stir fry another 2 minutes. Mix together and pour in:
   ¼ cup soy sauce
   1 tsp. sugar
   ¾ cup hot boullion

Stir fry another 2 minutes and serve over rice.

Per 1 ¼ Cup Serving: Calories: 221, Protein: 10 gm., Fat: 7 gm., Carbohydrates: 25 gm.

Angel Hair Primavera

Yield: 6 ½ cups

Cook according to package directions:
   12 oz. angel hair pasta or cappelini

Have ready:
   1 lb. zucchini, sliced
   6 oz. mushrooms, cut in quarters
   6 oz. snow peas, trimmed
   2 cups your favorite tomato sauce, heated

Heat in a wok or skillet:
2 Tbsp. oil

Add all the vegetables and stir fry about 5 minutes.

Add and toss in:
½ lb. tofu, cut in ½" cubes
salt

Serve on the angel hair pasta. Pass the tomato sauce and Parmesan cheese.

Per 1 Cup Serving: Calories: 250, Protein: 10 gm., Fat: 4 gm., Carbohydrates: 40 gm.

Tofu Tacos

Yield: 2 cups filling (4 tacos)

See photo, page 53.

Crumble into a bowl:
1 lb. tofu

Sprinkle with:
1-1 ¾ oz. pkg. taco seasoning mix

Mix this all together and then brown in:
2 Tbsp. oil

Serve on taco shells with the following fixings:
chopped tomatoes
lettuce
onion
grated cheese (optional)
hot sauce

Per ½ cup Serving: Calories: 73, Protein: 1 gm., Fat: 3 gm., Carbohydrate: 1 gm.

For Tostadas: Fry either corn or flour tortillas one at a time in hot oil until crisp and golden. Drain on paper toweling. To build the tostada, start with the crisp tortilla, then the seasoned tofu, chopped tomatoes, green peppers, and lettuce, then top with optional grated cheese and chopped olives. Spoon on hot sauce to taste.

Curry

Thaw, squeeze out and cut into bite size pieces:
>   **1 lb. frozen tofu**

Saute until transparent:
>   **2 Tbsp. oil**
>   **1 large onion, cut in half moons**
>   **2 cloves garlic, pressed**

Sprinkle over and stir in:
>   **2 Tbsp. unbleached white flour**
>   **1 ½ Tbsp. curry powder**
>   **½ tsp. freshly ground black pepper**

Then stir in:
>   **the bite size pieces of tofu**

Stir fry for a few minutes until the tofu starts to brown, then stir in:
>   **3 cups milk or soymilk**
>   **1 tsp. salt**

Continue stirring until just before it comes to a boil, then turn off the heat. Serve on rice with any any combination of yogurt, chutney, chopped peanuts, chopped cucumber, toasted coconut, and chopped green onions.

Per 1 ¼ Cup Serving: Calories: 295, Protein: 16 gm., Fat: 11 gm., Carbohydrates: 18 gm.

Chinese Fried Rice with Tofu

A good way to use leftover rice.

Have ready:
>   **2 cups cooked rice**
>   **½ lb. tofu, cut in small cubes**
>   **1 large onion, sliced**
>   **1 green pepper, sliced**
>   **2 ribs celery, sliced**
>   **2 green onions, with tops, cut in ½" pieces**

Heat in a wok or skillet:
2 Tbsp. oil

Add tofu cubes, and stir fry one minute, stir in the soy sauce. Remove the tofu, and add to the wok:
2 Tbsp. oil

Add the onion, celery, and green pepper and stir fry for 3-4 minutes. Crumble in the cooked rice and stir fry 2 minutes.

Stir in the tofu plus:
1 Tbsp. soy sauce

Serve topped with the green onions.

Per 1 Cup Serving: Calories: 289, Protein: 7 gm., Fat: 14 gm., Carbohydrates: 28 gm.

Deviled Tofu

Yield: 4 servings

Have ready:
1 lb. tofu, cut in 8 slices
2 cups fresh bread crumbs (can be made in the food processor or blender from day old bread)

Mix in a shallow dish:
½ cup Dijon mustard
½ cup green onions, with tops, cut small
1 tsp. thyme
¼ tsp. black pepper

Melt in a skillet:
¼ cup margarine or butter
¼ cup oil

Take 2 Tbsp. of the oil mixture and stir into the mustard sauce. Dip tofu slices into the sauce, coating evenly, then into the crumbs, patting crumbs on. Brown the coated tofu slices on each side in the skillet.

Per Slice: Calories: 170, Protein: 5 gm., Fat: 8 gm., Carbohydrates: 4 gm.

Pizza with Tofu

Yield: 6 slices

Preheat oven to 450° F.

Have ready:
1-10" ready-made pizza crust

Spread with:
1 cup your favorite tomato sauce

Sprinkle over the top:
½ lb. tofu, crumbled
1 cup mushrooms, sliced
½ cup olives, sliced
½ cup mozzarella, grated

Bake for about 15 minutes or until cheese is melted.

Per Slice: Calories: 362, Protein: 15 gm., Fat: 3 gm., Carbohydrates: 58 gm.

Pesto Pizza

Yield: 8 pieces

Have ready:
1-12" ready-made pizza crust
1½ cups Pesto Dip or Spread, p. 25

Preheat oven to 450° F.

Spread the Pesto Spread evenly over the pizza crust, then top with:
1 cup mushrooms, sliced
½ cup olives, sliced
1 small sweet onion, cut in rings

Bake about 10 to 15 minutes and serve.

Per Slice: Calories: 234, Protein: 8 gm., Fat: 3 gm., Carbohydrates: 28 gm.

Pizza Burritos

Yield: 12 burritos

Preheat oven to 350° F.

Have ready:
   1 lb. frozen tofu, thawed, squeezed dry,
      then cubed or torn into bite size pieces
   12-8″ flour tortillas

Saute together:
   2 Tbsp. oil
   1 medium onion, chopped (1 ¼ cups)
   ½ green pepper, chopped (¾ cup)

While the onion and pepper are cooking put tofu pieces in a bowl and add:
   ¾ cup olives, sliced (black, green or mixed)
   1-4.5 oz. jar sliced mushrooms, drained
   1-16 oz. can pizza sauce
   ½ tsp. salt

Add the onions and peppers and mix all together. Heat each tortilla for a few seconds on a hot griddle, just until soft. Put ½ cup of the tofu mixture in the center of each tortilla as it comes off the griddle and fold up like an envelope. Place on an oiled cookie sheet, brush the tops with oil and bake for about 10 minutes.

Per Burrito: Calories: 102, Protein: 4 gm., Fat: 2 gm., Carbohydrates: 7 gm.

Golden Rice Pilaf

Yield: 5 cups

Saute in a 2 quart saucepan until softened:
2 Tbsp. oil
1 medium onion, chopped

Stir in and cook for 2 minutes to coat:
1 cup long grain rice

Add:
2 ½ cups hot vegetable boullion   ½ tsp. corriander
½ cup raisins   ½ tsp. curry powder
½ tsp. tumeric   ½ tsp. salt

Stir, cover and cook over low heat 10 to 12 minutes until most of the liquid is absorbed.

Remove from heat and fluff into the rice:
½ lb. tofu, cut in ½" cubes

Cover and let sit 10 minutes. Add and fluff in:
½ cup slivered, toasted almonds

Serve with a sprinkle of minced parsley.

Per Serving: Calories: 314, Protein: 9 gm., Fat: 8 gm., Carbohydrates: 36 gm.

Burritos Fritos

Yield: 8 burritos

Have ready:
2-4 oz. cans whole green chiles
8 oz. Cheddar or Monterey Jack cheese
½ lb. tofu, cut in 8 sticks
8 large flour tortillas

Soften each tortilla on a hot griddle. Lay out one seeded green chile in the middle of each tortilla, top with one slice of cheese, then one tofu stick. Fold up like an envelope, then fry in hot oil until golden on both sides. Serve hot with salsa.

Per Burrito: Calories: 308, Protein: 11 gm., Fat: 20 gm., Carbohydrates: 11 gm.

Sloppy Joes

Yield: 3 ½ cups

Sloppy Joe can be served in toasted buns, mixed in with elbow macaroni, over spaghetti or rice.

Saute together in a 10″ skillet:
2 Tbsp. oil
1 medium onion, diced
1 small green pepper

Mix together in a bowl:
1 lb. tofu, crumbled
2 Tbsp. soy sauce

Add the tofu mixture to the cooking onions and peppers, and continue cooking until the tofu starts to brown.

Stir in:
2 cups your favorite tomato sauce
1 Tbsp. chili powder

Per ½ Cup Serving: Calories: 119, Protein: 7 gm., Fat: 4 gm., Carbohydrates: 10 gm.

For a Quicker Sloppy Joe:
Start by browning the tofu sprinkled with soy sauce in 2 tbsp. oil, then add a 15 oz. can of prepared Sloppy Joe sauce, or a 1.5 oz. package dry flavoring mix for Sloppy Joe along with a 6 oz. can tomato paste and a cup of water.

Spinach Triangles

Yield: 12 triangles

Have ready:
   1-1 lb. pkg. fillo leaves, thawed
   1-10 oz. pkg. frozen chopped spinach, thawed and drained

Saute together:
   2 Tbsp. oil
   1 large onion, chopped

When the onions are transparent, mix together with:
   1 lb. tofu, crumbled   **½ tsp. black pepper**
   the thawed and drained spinach   **½ tsp. garlic powder**
   1 tsp. salt

Melt:
   ¾ lb. margarine or butter

Have everything ready before opening up the package of fillo leaves.
Take 2 (14 ″ X 18″) fillo leaves, one on top of the other for each triangle.
Brush with 1 Tbsp. melted margarine or butter, then fold in half to
make a 9″ X 14″ piece. Put ⅓ cup filling at the bottom and turn the
leaves up about ¾″ from the bottom and the two sides. Then fold the
lower corner on an angle to start the triangle shape. Continue to fold
up like a flag until the triangle is formed. Place on a margarined or
buttered cookie sheet and bake about 15 to 20 minutes until browned
and crisp.

Per Triangle: Calories: 263, Protein: 7 gm., Fat: 7 gm., Carbohydrates: 24 gm.

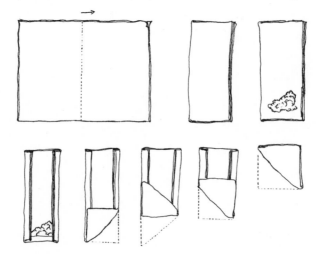

Desserts

Almond Cheescake ◆ 84
Apricot Pudding ◆ 88
Blueberry Cheesecake ◆ 84
Cheesecake ◆ 84
Cherry Cheesecake ◆ 84
Cherry Cobbler ◆ 87
Cherry Pudding ◆ 90
Chewy Brown Sugar Bars ◆ 86
Creamy Chocolate Marble Pie ◆ 90
Creamy Cookie Pudding ◆ 88
Creamy Mint Cookie Pudding ◆ 88
Creamy Topping ◆ 93
Creamy Topping with Honey ◆ 93
Fresh Fruit Pudding ◆ 89
Fresh Orange Pudding ◆ 89
Fruit Cocktail Pudding ◆ 89
Gingersnap-Lemon Ice Box Cake ◆ 91
Half and Half Cheesecake ◆ 85
Maple Pecan Cheesecake ◆ 85
Pecan Pie ◆ 92
Pineapple Ice Box Cake ◆ 91
Raspberry Pudding ◆ 89
Strawberries and Creamy Topping in Patty Shells ◆ 92
Vanilla Rolled Cookies ◆ 86

Cheesecake

Yield: one 8" cheesecake

See photo on back cover.

Preheat oven to 350° F.

Have ready:
1-8" graham cracker crust, unbaked

Blend in a food processor until smooth and creamy:

1 lb. tofu	**2 Tbsp. lemon juice**
½ cup brown sugar	**1 Tbsp. unbleached white flour**
⅓ cup honey	**1 tsp. vanilla**
¼ cup oil	**pinch of salt**

Pour into the unbaked pie shell and bake for about 45 minutes or until cracks start to form around the edge of the filling.

Per Serving: Calories: 424, Protein: 7 gm., Fat: 13 gm., Carbohydrates: 59 gm.

Cherry or Blueberry Cheesecake: Fold in 1½ cups pitted cherries or blueberries.

Almond Cheesecake

Yield: one 8" cheesecake

Preheat oven to 350° F.

Have ready:
one 8" graham cracker crust, unbaked

Blend in a food processor until smooth and creamy:

1 lb. tofu	**¼ cup oil**
½ cup brown sugar	**2 Tbsp. lemon juice**
½ cup almond meal	**1 tsp. almond extract**
¼ cup honey	**pinch of salt**

Pour into the unbaked pie shell and bake for about 45 minutes or until cracks start to form on the edge of the filling.

Per Serving: Calories: 465, Protein: 9 gm., Fat: 14 gm., Carbohydrates: 57 gm.

Half and Half Cheesecake

Yield: one 8" cheesecake

Preheat oven to 350° F.

Have ready:
one 8" graham cracker crust, unbaked

Blend in a food processor until smooth and creamy:
8 oz. tofu
8 oz. cream cheese
½ cup brown sugar
⅓ cup honey
2 Tbsp. lemon juice
1 tsp. vanilla
pinch of salt

Pour into the unbaked pie shell and bake for about 45 minutes.

Per Serving: Calories: 436, Protein: 7 gm., Fat: 12 gm., Carbohydrates: 58 gm.

Maple Pecan Cheesecake

Yield: one 8" cheesecake

Preheat oven to 350° F.

Have ready:
one 8" graham cracker crust, unbaked

Blend in a food processor until smooth and creamy:
1 lb. tofu
1 cup maple syrup
2 Tbsp. margarine
pinch of salt

Fold in:
½ cup broken pecan pieces

Pour into the unbaked pie shell and bake for about 45 minutes or until cracks start to appear around the edge of the filling. Serve cold, topped with maple syrup and pecans or Creamy Topping, page 93.

Per Serving: Calories: 438, Protein: 8 gm., Fat: 8 gm., Carbohydrates: 60 gm.

Chewy Brown Sugar Bars

Yield: 2 dozen bars

Preheat oven to 350° F.

Blend together in a food processor until smooth and creamy:
**½ lb. soft tofu
1 cup brown sugar
½ cup margarine
1 tsp. vanilla**

Mix together in a bowl:
**2 cups unbleached white flour
1 cup pecan meal
   or 1 cup whole wheat flour
1 ½ tsp. baking powder
½ tsp. baking soda
½ tsp. salt**

Add the dry ingredients to the creamy tofu mixture in the food processor and pulse 8-10 times or just until blended. Spread or pat into a 9" x 13" pan and bake 20 to 25 minutes, until browned.

Per Bar: Calories: 139, Protein: 4 gm., Fat: 2 gm., Carbohydrates: 17 gm.

Variations: Fold in one of the following; **1 cup chocolate chips,** 1 cup raisins, ¾ **cup cranberries** or ¾ **cup blueberries** with either ½ **cup walnuts, pecans or other nuts.**

Vanilla Rolled Cookies

Yield: About 30 3" cookies

Preheat oven to 350° F.

Cream together in a food processor:
**¾ cup brown sugar
½ cup margarine
¼ lb. soft tofu
2 tsp. vanilla**

Mix together in a bowl:
  3 cups unbleached white flour
  2 tsp. baking powder
  ½ tsp. salt

Add the dry ingredients to the wet and pulse only until blended (about 10 pulses).

Roll out ¼" thick and cut in shapes. Bake for 8-10 minutes.

Per cookie: Calories: 90, Protein: 1 gm., Fat: 1 gm., Carbohydrates: 14 gm.

Cherry Cobbler

Yield: 9 servings

Preheat oven to 375° F.

Blend together in a food processor:
  1 cup flour
  1 tsp. baking powder

Add while the processor is running:
  ¼ lb. tofu
  2 Tbsp. oil
  ½ cup milk or soymilk
  ⅓ cup sugar

Process only until the dough is just blended, then spread it in an oiled 8" X 8" pan.

Cover with:
  1-17 oz. can pitted sweetened dark cherries,
    drained with juice reserved

Heat the reserved cherry juice to a boil and pour over all.

Bake 40 to 45 minutes and serve warm.

Per Serving: Calories: 160, Protein: 3 gm., Fat: 3 gm., Carbohydrates: 28 gm.

Creamy Cookie Pudding

Yield: About 2½ cups

See photo, page 72.

Blend in a food processor or blender until smooth and creamy:
½ lb.tofu
⅓ cup sugar
2 Tbsp. oil
1 tsp. vanilla
pinch of salt

Break into quarters:
8 chocolate sandwich cookies with vanilla filling

Fold the cookie pieces into the pudding and chill 2 hours to overnight.

Per ½ Cup Serving: Calories: 193, Protein: 4 gm., Fat: 8 gm., Carbohydrates: 22 gm.

Creamy Mint Cookie Pudding: Use chocolate
sandwich cookies with mint flavored filling.

Apricot Pudding

Yield: About 3 cups

See photo, page 72.

Blend together in a food processor or blender:
½ lb. tofu
¼ cup honey or sugar
2 Tbsp. oil

Add and blend in:
1-20 oz. can apricot halves, drained
(you can reserve a few halves for garnish)

Pour into serving dishes, chill and serve.

Per ½ Cup Serving: Calories: 152, Protein: 4 gm., Fat: 5 gm., Carbohydrates: 23 gm.

Raspberry Pudding

Yield: 2 cups

See photo, page 72.

Blend in a food processor or blender until smooth and creamy:
> **5 oz. frozen raspberries in light syrup**
> **(you can reserve a few whole berries for garnish)**
> **½ lb. tofu**
> **¼ cup sugar or 3 Tbsp. honey**
> **pinch of salt**

Pour into serving dishes and chill.

Per ½ Cup Serving: Calories: 122, Protein: 5 gm., Fat: 0 gm., Carbohydrates: 22 gm.

Fresh Orange Pudding

Yield: About 4 cups

Have ready:
> **2 navel oranges, cut in bite size pieces**

Blend in a food processor or blender until smooth and creamy:
> **½ lb. tofu**
> **¼ cup oil**
> **¼ cup honey or sugar**
> **1 tsp. vanilla**
> **pinch of salt**

Fold orange pieces in and serve at once.

Per ½ Cup Serving: Calories: 123, Protein: 2 gm., Fat: 7 gm., Carbohydrates: 11 gm.

Fresh Fruit Pudding: Substitute **any fresh fruit cut in bite size pieces for the navel oranges.**

Fruit Cocktail Pudding: Substitute **2 cups drained fruit cocktail for the navel oranges.**

Cherry Pudding

Yield: 2 cups

Blend in a food processor or blender until smooth and creamy:
½ lb. tofu
½ lb. dark sweet pitted cherries
¼ cup sugar or 3 Tbsp. honey
pinch of salt

Pour into serving dishes and chill.

Per ½ Cup Serving: Calories: 124, Protein: 5 gm., Fat: 0 gm., Carbohydrates: 22 gm.

Creamy Chocolate Marble Pie

Yield: One 8" pie

Have ready:
one 8" graham cracker crust, baked

Blend together in a food processor or blender until smooth and creamy:
1 lb. tofu
⅔ cup sugar
¼ cup oil
2 tsp. vanilla
pinch of salt

Spread all but one cup of this mixture in the baked pie shell.

Add to the 1 cup left in the food processor:
3 Tbsp. cocoa

Process until mixed in, then drop spoonfuls of the chocolate into the vanilla. Swirl the two together with a knife and chill until firm.

Per Serving: Calories: 409, Protein: 7 gm., Fat: 13 gm., Carbohydrates: 54 gm.

Gingersnap-Lemon Ice Box Cake

Yield: 9 Servings

Have ready:
1½ cups Creamy Topping, p. 93

Cover the bottom of an 8" X 8" cake pan with:
14 gingersnaps, broken into crumbs

Spread over these:
1-20 oz. can lemon pie filling

Cover with the Creamy Topping, then sprinkle with:
12 gingersnaps, crushed

Refrigerate at least 4 hours or overnight until firm.

Per Serving: Calories:295, Protein: 5 gm., Fat: 9 gm., Carbohydrates: 43 gm.

Pineapple Ice Box Cake

Yield: 9 servings

Crush in a paper bag or food processor:
1-10 oz. pkg. sugar wafer cookies

Reserve half the crumbs for topping and sprinkle half on the bottom of a 9" X 9" pan.

Have ready:
1-20 oz. can crushed pineapple, reserving juice

Blend in a food processor or blender until smooth and creamy:
1 lb. tofu
½ cup oil
½ cup sugar
¼ cup lemon juice
the reserved pineapple juice

Pour onto the crumbs, top with the crushed pineapple, and sprinkle the reserved crumbs over the top. Chill at least 4 hours or overnight until firm.

Per Serving: Calories: 383, Protein: 6 gm., Fat: 19 gm., Carbohydrates: 45 gm.

Strawberries and Creamy Topping In Patty Shells

Yield: 6 Servings

Bake according to package directions:
6 frozen patty shells

While they are baking, prepare:
1½ cups Creamy Topping, p. 93

Wash and trim:
2 pints strawberries

Stir into the berries:
½ cup sugar

Fill each cooled patty shell with Creamy Topping, then spoon strawberries over the top.

Per Serving: Calories: 407, Protein: 5 gm., Fat: 20 gm., Carbohydrates: 39 gm.

Pecan Pie

Yield: 8 servings

Preheat oven to 350° F.

Have ready:
one unbaked 8″ pie crust

Blend in a food processor until smooth and creamy:
½ lb. tofu   **¼ cup margarine**
1 cup brown sugar   **1 tsp. vanilla**
⅓ cup sorghum molasses   **¼ tsp. salt**

Fold in:
1 ½ cups whole pecan pieces

Pour into the unbaked pie shell and bake for about 45 minutes or until cracks start to form around the edge of the filling. Serve with Creamy Topping, p 93., or vanilla ice cream.

Per Serving: Calories: 424, Protein: 5 gm., Fat: 12 gm., Carbohydrates: 44 gm.

Creamy Topping

Yield: 1 ½ cups

Blend in a food processor or blender until smooth and creamy:
   ½ **lb. tofu**
   ¼ **cup oil**
   ¼ **cup confectioners sugar**
   1 **tsp. vanilla**
   ½ **tsp. lemon juice**
   ⅛ **tsp. salt**

Chill and serve as you would whipped cream.

Per 2 Tbsp. Serving: Calories: 78, Protein: 2 gm., Fat: 5 gm., Carbohydrates: 4 gm.

Creamy Topping With Honey

Yield: 1 ½ cups

Blend in a food processor or blender until smooth and creamy:
   ½ **lb. tofu**
   ¼ **cup oil**
   2 **Tbsp. honey**
   ½ **Tbsp. lemon juice**
   ½ **tsp. vanilla**
   ¼ **tsp. salt**

Chill and serve as you would whipped cream.

Per 2 Tbsp. Serving: Calories: 78, Protein: 2 gm., Fat: 5 gm., Carbohydrates: 4 gm.

Recipe Index

A

Aguacate, Ensalada de, 29
Almond Cheescake, 84
Amandine Tofu, 61
Angel Hair Primavera, 74
Apple Kuchen, 12
Apple Pancakes, 12
Apricot Pudding, 88
Avocado Salad, 29
Avocado Salad, Stuffed, 38

B

Barbecue Tofu, 57
Bars, Chewy Brown Sugar, 86
Basil-Garlic Dressing, 41
Bean Salad, Four, 39
Bean Salad, Garbanzo, 32
Bean Salad, Pinto, 30
Blue Cheese Spread, 24
Blueberry Cheesecake, 84
Blueberry Pancakes, 12
Boofers, 16
Broccoli Quiche, 10
Broccoli-Mushroom Stir Fry, 64
Brown Sugar Bars, Chewy, 86
Brunch, 10-16
Burgers, Tofu, 56
Burritos Fritos, 80
Burritos, Pizza, 79

C

Cabbage Tofu Stir Fry, 62
Cashew Spread, 21
Cheese, Lasagne with, 67
Cheesecake, 84
Cheesecakes, 84-85
Cherry Cheesecake, 84
Cherry Cobbler, 87
Cherry Pudding, 90
Chewy Brown Sugar Bars, 86
Chicken Salad, Mock, 32
Chile Quiles, 64
Chili, Southwestern, 48
Chinese Fried Rice with Tofu, 76
Chocolate Marble Pie, Creamy, 90
Chowder, Corn, 47

Chunky Gazpacho, 50
Chutney Dip, Curry, 22
Chutney Dressing, 41
Cobbler, Cherry, 87
Cold Curried Rice Salad, 33
Cole Slaw Dressing, 44
Cookie Pudding, Creamy, 88
Cookies, Vanilla Rolled, 86
Corn Chowder, 47
Creamy Chocolate Marble Pie, 90
Creamy Cookie Pudding, 88
Creamy Mint Cookie Pudding, 88
Creamy Salad Dressing, 42
Creamy Topping, 93
Creamy Topping with Honey, 93
Cruise Ship Mustard Dressing, 44
Cucumber Dill Dip, 24
Cucumber-Dill Dressing, 44
Cucumber-Dill Salad, 33
Curried Rice Salad, Cold, 33
Curry, 76
Curry Chutney Dip, 22
Curry Dressing, 43

D

Desserts, 84-93
Deviled Tofu, 77
Dill Dip, Cucumber, 24
Dill Dressing, Cucumber-, 44
Dill Salad, Cucumber, 33
Dips, 20-26
Dressings, 41-44
Dry Onion Soup Dip, 22
Dry Onion-Tomato Soup Dip, 22
Dry Vegetable Soup Dip, 22

E

Enchilada Casserole, 65
Ensalada de Aguacate, 29

F

Far East Dip, 21
Florentine, Lasagne, 66
Four Bean Salad, 39
Fresh Fruit Pudding, 89
Fresh Orange Pudding, 89
Fried Rice with Tofu, 13
Fried Tofu, Oven, 58
Fried Tofu, Quick and Easy, 56
Fritos, Burritos, 80

Fruit Cocktail Pudding, 89
Fruit Pudding, Fresh, 89
Fruit Salad Dressing, Mom's, 42

G

Garbanzo Bean Salad, 32
Garlic Lo-Cal Dressing, 43
Gazpacho, Chunky, 50
Gingersnap-Lemon Ice Box
   Cake, 91
Golden Rice, 80
Green Dip or Spread, 20
Green Goddess Dip, 26
Green Rice, 60
Gumbo Soup, 46

H

Half and Half Cheesecake, 85
Hash Browns, 16
Hawaiian Stir Fry, 70
Herb Dip, 25
Horseradish Dip, 20
Hot Pink Dip, 20

I

Ice Box Cakes, 91
Iowa Potato Salad, 38

J

Jumbo Shells, Stuffed, 62

K

Kuchen, Apple, 12

L

Lasagne, 66
Lasagne Florentine, 66
Lasagne with Cheese, 67
Lebanese Salad for Pita Pockets,
   31
Lemon Ice Box Cake, Ginger-
   snap, 91
Lentil Soup, 52
Lo-Cal Dressing, Garlic, 43
Lo-Cal Dressing, Pink, 43
Loaf, Tofu, 57

M

Macaroni and Tofu and Cheese,
   60
Maple Pecan Cheesecake, 85
Marble Pie, Creamy Chocolate,
   90
Mexicali Rice Bake, 15

Mint Cookie Pudding, Creamy,
   88
Miso Vegetable Soup, 49
Mock Chicken Salad, 32
Mock Sour Cream Dressing, 42
Mock Vichysoisse, 52
Mom's Fruit Salad Dressing, 42
Mushroom Quiche, 10
Mushroom Scrambled Tofu, 14
Mustard Dressing, Cruise Ship,
   44

N

Noodle Soup, Ramen, 48
Noodles Romanoff, 73

O

Olive-Pecan Spread, 23
Onion Soup Dip, Dry, 22
Onion-Tomato Soup Dip, Dry, 22
Orange Pudding, Fresh, 89
Orange Tofu, 59
Oriental Stir Fry, 74
Oven Fried Tofu, 58

P

Pancakes, 12
Pasta Salad, Pepper-, 39
Pasta-Tofu Salad, 37
Patty Shells, Creamy Topping
   and Strawberries, 92
Peanut Slaw, Pineapple-, 29
Pecan Pie, 92
Pecan Spread, Olive-, 23
Pepper-Pasta Salad, 39
Pesto Dip or Spread, 25
Pesto Pizza, 78
Pie, Pecan, 92
Pine Nut Salad, Spinach-, 30
Pineapple Ice Box Cake, 91
Pineapple-Peanut Slaw, 29
Pink Lo-Cal Dressing, 43
Pinto Bean Salad, 30
Pita Pockets, Lebanese Salad for,
   31
Pizza Burritos, 79
Pizza with Tofu, 78
Pizza, Pesto, 78
Potato Salad, Iowa, 38
Potato Tofu Soup, 52
Puddings, 88-90
Pumpkin Soup, 51

Q

Quiche, Broccoli, 10
Quiche, Mushroom, 10
Quick and Easy Fried Tofu, 56
Quick Vegetable Tofu Soup, 46

R

Ramen Noodle Soup, 48
Rancheros, Scrambled Tofu, 15
Raspberry Pudding, 89
Rice Bake, Mexicali, 15
Rice Salad, Cold Curried, 33
Rice, Fried with Tofu, 13
Rice, Green, 60
Rice, Spanish, 11
Rolled Cookies, Vanilla, 86
Rolls, Spring, 68

S

Salad Dressings, 41-44
Salads, 28-40
Sauce, Tartar, 23
Scrambled Tofu, 14
Scrambled Tofu Rancheros, 15
Scrambled Tofu, Mushroom, 14
Seashell Salad, 37
Sesame Spinach Salad, 40
Shells, Stuffed Jumbo, 62
Sloppy Joes, 81
Soup Dips, 22
Soups, 46-52
Sour Cream Dressing, Mock, 42
Southwestern Chili, 48
Spaghetti Balls, Tofu, 57
Spanish Rice, 11
Spinach Salad, Sesame, 40
Spinach Soup, 50
Spinach Triangles, 82

Spinach-Pine Nut Salad, 30
Spreads, 20-25
Spring Rolls, 68
Stir Fry, Broccoli-Mushroom, 64
Stir Fry, Cabbage Tofu, 62
Stir Fry, Hawaiian, 70
Stir Fry, Oriental, 74
Strawberries and Creamy
    Topping in Patty Shells, 92
Stroganoff, 63
Stuffed Avocado Salad, 38
Stuffed Jumbo Shells, 62

T

Taco Salad, 28
Tacos, Tofu, 75
Tamale Pie, 69
Tartar Sauce, 23
Tofu Burgers, 56
Tofu Loaf, 57
Tofu Salad No.1, 34
Tofu Salad No.2, 34
Tofu Spaghetti Balls, 57
Tofu Tacos, 75
Tofu, Fried Rice with, 13
Tofu, Pizza with, 78
Toppings, 93
Tostadas, 75
Triangles, Spinach, 82

V

Vanilla Rolled Cookies, 86
Vegetable Soup Dip, Dry, 22
Vegetable Soup, Miso, 49
Vegetable Tofu Soup, Quick, 46
Vichysoisse, Mock, 52

W

Waldorf Salad, 31

Nutritional Analyses

Each of the recipes in this book have been analyzed for their calorie count and protein, fat and carbohydrate content. Items that were not included in these analyses were variations listed at the end of a recipe, garnishes, or supplimentary foods suggested to compliment the recipes in a meal, such as potatoes or rice. If a choice of ingredients was given in a recipe, the first ingredient listed was the one used in the nutritional analysis.